A YEAR OF SELF-ESTEEM

A YEAR OF
Self-Esteem

DAILY REFLECTIONS AND PRACTICES FOR EMBRACING YOUR WORTH

JUDITH BELMONT, MS

ROCKRIDGE
PRESS

Series Designer: Alyssa Nassner
Interior and Cover Designer: Sean Doyle
Art Producer: Sara Feinstein
Editor: Samantha Holland
Production Editor: Nora Milman

All illustration used under license from iStock.com.

Paperback ISBN: 978-1-63807-340-6 | eBook ISBN: 978-1-63807-138-9
R0

To my clients and the readers of my previous books
who have trusted me in their self-esteem journey.

Contents

Self-esteem comes from being able to define the world in your own terms and refusing to abide by the judgments of others.

—OPRAH WINFREY

Introduction

Welcome! Thank you for joining this journey toward loving yourself once and for all.

If you chose to read this book, chances are you are looking for support, information, and strategies to build your self-esteem, love yourself, and love your life.

Self-esteem refers to the basic relationship you have with yourself. If you have nagging self-doubt, are self-critical, or look to others for approval more than you do yourself, your self-esteem will be low, and your self-confidence will be shaky. Conversely, if you have a high degree of self-confidence and feelings of self-worth, you will be satisfied with yourself and your self-esteem will flourish.

This book offers a mix of simple practices, reflections, affirmations, and inspirational quotes to help you on your path to improving your self-esteem. You will find various ways to get rid of that critical voice inside your head that reminds you more of your shortcomings than your successes. You'll also learn information and practical tools to shift your focus away from past mistakes and regrets toward your courage, uniqueness, and inherent beauty. Whether you are looking for a self-esteem tune-up or a major overhaul, this book can serve as your guide to improved self-confidence and unconditional self-acceptance.

Low self-esteem is a universal issue many people struggle with to varying degrees. I should know. Growing up as a sensitive, gawky girl who was a head taller than almost anyone in my class, I was crippled by painful shyness. Now, 50 years and many life experiences later, it's hard for me to remember being that girl who could not find her voice to speak up in class. Even my young adult self would not have believed that, many years later, I would have the insight to write this book and the confidence to express myself without worrying about what people thought.

It wasn't an easy road. I had to work hard at developing my self-esteem. I am a living testament that low self-esteem is not a life sentence. It is something that can be changed to make you a self-loving, confident person who is satisfied with yourself and your life.

This book is about moving forward. It is not about blaming yourself or others for how you got here. Sure, the past might offer useful information, but looking back just long enough to learn from it is a helpful way to move ahead with empowerment and confidence.

My degree in clinical psychology and my work as a psychotherapist and online mental health coach have helped me learn the ropes of improving self-esteem through widely accepted psychological treatment practices. I have been struck by how low self-esteem colors my clients' view of themselves and their world, distorting their perceptions and leading to depression and anxiety. They trust me to share their struggles and their successes as they throw off the chains from the past that have held them back for so long, and eventually embrace their greatness and beauty without reservation.

As the author of eight books and two therapeutic card decks, I have offered therapists, clients, and self-help lovers tips and tools to build self-esteem. In this book, I continue to build upon topics I've written about in the past, such as healthy thinking skills, optimism, assertiveness, overcoming regret, gratitude, forgiveness, thriving under stress, coping skills, and mindfulness.

While this book offers useful information, it is no substitute for professional help if your struggles with self-esteem are significantly impairing your life and leading to symptoms of mental health issues such as anxiety and depression. If you're struggling with these issues, please seek out a mental health or medical professional to help you get to a place where you can more effectively use this book to improve yourself and your life.

Whether you are a young adult or more senior, these reflections, short practices, positive affirmations, and powerful quotes will help you silence your self-doubt. Giving yourself 10 to 15 minutes a day to commit to each daily entry, no matter when you start in the year, will provide you with structure on your self-esteem journey. Consider keeping a journal to reflect and review as needed. Also, if any daily entries are especially relevant, refer back to those key concepts and practices to solidify your growth and learning. You alone know what you need the most.

Thank you for allowing me to help you become the most authentic and beautiful YOU that you can be. I hope that through this process you will see yourself as loving and worthy of love, with no strings attached. May you silence that nagging, critical voice in your head once and for all, and may you only listen to your words of self-compassion, kindness, and love. You deserve it!

JANUARY

1
JANUARY

GIVE YOURSELF A FRESH START

You don't have to wait for the new year to start fresh. Commit to starting each day this year with a new positive intention, such as "Today I will choose an attitude of gratitude."

2
JANUARY

DAILY AFFIRMATIONS

Affirmations are soothing statements you tell yourself as a reminder of your worth. Think of an affirmation that provides words of encouragement, such as "What I have to say is valuable," and put it into action by expressing yourself confidently to others. Try coming up with a new affirmation every day this year and write each one down in a notebook or on a piece of paper. Refer to your growing list frequently to remind yourself of your worth.

3

FORGIVE AND REFLECT

Forgiving yourself and others can be hard, but it is one of the most important gifts you can give yourself. Consider replacing the adage "forgive and forget" with "forgive and reflect." After all, why would you ever want to forget your most important lessons?

4

JANUARY

LEARN FROM FAILURE

The road to success is paved with setbacks and failures. Don't define yourself by your missteps; instead, be motivated by them.

5

JANUARY

BITE-SIZE RESOLUTIONS

Make your resolutions and goals achievable by breaking them up into small chunks, or mini-habits. If your goal is to walk 10,000 steps a day, set yourself up for success by starting with a minimum of 500 or 1,000 steps per day when life gets busy. What other goals can you make bite-size?

6

JANUARY

LEAVE FOOTPRINTS OF KINDNESS

Kindness is a way to show your gratitude toward others. Wherever you go and whatever you do, strive to always leave footprints of kindness.

7

JANUARY

SELF-ESTEEM TOOL KIT

Assemble a tool kit to remind yourself of your worth when you're feeling down. Find a container and fill it with items that represent self-love to you. For example, a polished stone might remind you of how special you are, or a pencil may represent how you create your life story. Include note cards with inspirational quotes or affirmations to give you strength. What else would be helpful to add?

8

JANUARY

LOVE YOURSELF ABOVE ALL

To love oneself is the beginning of a lifelong romance.

—OSCAR WILDE

9

ARE YOU AN APPROVAL CHASER?

Do you seek approval from others more than you seek your own? No amount of approval from someone else can replace your own self-love.

10

KEEP A SELF-ESTEEM JOURNAL

As you read an entry each day, consider keeping a Self-Esteem Journal. This journal will give you a place to respond to the practices and reflections in this book. You can review your responses from time to time to see how you've grown and remind yourself of issues that still need to be addressed.

11

JANUARY

FORGIVENESS DOESN'T MEAN CONDONING

Even if someone wrongs you, forgive them anyway. You don't deserve to be mired in negativity. But it doesn't mean you should go back for more!

12

JANUARY

START THE DAY OFF RIGHT

Starting the day with words of encouragement will help you stay positive and boost your self-esteem. Think of something personal that will offer you just what you need in the moment, like "I am a good person and worthy of love" or "I will create a beautiful day." Consider writing your words of encouragement in your journal to start the day, and repeat them throughout the day to keep them at the forefront of your mind.

13

JANUARY

LIFE IS LIKE SWISS CHEESE

Swiss cheese is full of holes, which makes it distinctive. Just like Swiss cheese, the holes and challenges in our lives give us character and depth. So, embrace your imperfections; they make you unique.

14

JANUARY

THE MIND-BODY CONNECTION

Start the new year by improving your physical health as well as your mindset. Write down your goals for both areas and make them as specific as possible. For example, *Read a self-help book for 5 minutes in the morning* or *Take a 10-minute walk every day.* Writing your goals down makes it more likely that you will commit to them and succeed in making them daily habits.

15

JANUARY

—

PERFECTION AND SELF-ESTEEM DON'T MIX

Perfection gives you little room for error. Instead of trying to be perfect, try being authentic. How would it feel to be perfectly you?

16

JANUARY

—

CHOOSE A GROWTH MINDSET

Take some time today to focus on choosing a growth mindset. Don't define yourself by your imperfections, but by your motivation and efforts to overcome them. Focus on what you can do now. For example, a fixed mindset might sound like "I can't express myself without fear of sounding silly," whereas a growth mindset sounds like "I am learning how to find my voice and express my opinions."

17

APPROVE OF YOURSELF

Remember, you have been criticizing yourself for years, and it hasn't worked. Try approving of yourself and see what happens.

—LOUISE HAY

18

AN AFFIRMATION FOR THOUGHTS AND FEELINGS

I am the gatekeeper of my thoughts and feelings—no one can control them without my permission.

19

JANUARY

RELABEL YOUR THOUGHTS

Negative labels you apply to yourself like "too sensitive" or "lazy" can damage self-confidence. Less judgmental thoughts might be "I have a hard time getting motivated" or "I tend to take things personally." Physically relabel your thoughts with this practice: Find some adhesive labels or stickers and write down any negative thoughts that impact your self-esteem. Then, put new labels over the negative ones with more positive thoughts written on them. Place them some-where prominent, like in your journal or on the refrigerator so you see them often.

20

JANUARY

REFUSE TO COLLECT INJUSTICES

When you hold grudges, you end up collecting injustices, leaving you bitter and angry. Allow forgiveness and gratitude into your life once and for all.

21

JANUARY

DEVELOP A SELF-CARE RITUAL

Rituals help healthy behaviors become a regular part of our self-care practice. Rituals can be as simple as maintaining a stretching or walking routine, sipping a cup of coffee in the morning, reading the news, or writing a positive intention for the day. Are there any self-care rituals that you would like to incorporate into your life? Make a "Self-Care Ritual" log for a week or more to help you keep track of what works and what doesn't.

22

JANUARY

REVIEW, REFLECT, AND RENEW

What hurt you, helped you, or made you wiser last year? How can you learn from your setbacks? With renewed purpose after reviewing and reflecting, build on what you did yesterday for a better tomorrow.

23

JANUARY

BELIEVE IN YOURSELF

Believe in yourself, your goodness, and your beauty. If others invalidate you, it says a lot more about them than it does you.

24
JANUARY

USE COPING STATEMENTS

When you feel your self-esteem start to decline, make a list of coping statements that remind you of healthy thoughts and skills that support you. Something like "My opinion of myself is more important than anyone else's" or "I have faith in myself that I can get through this." Keep this list handy in your wallet, on your desktop screensaver, or even as an electronic sticky note on your computer.

25
JANUARY

SOW KINDNESS

Plant seeds of kindness wherever you go. You will reap so much more than you sow.

26

CHOOSE SELF-COMPASSION

Although it is often thought that self-esteem is gained through success, research has shown that the key to self-esteem is through self-compassion because it allows you to be kind to yourself, boosting your feelings of self-worth. Practice improving your self-esteem by transforming critical self-talk into compassionate self-talk. For example, "I can't believe I screwed up the relationship" could be transformed into "I tried my best and forgive myself for not knowing then what I know now."

27

AN AFFIRMATION FOR TODAY

Today is the day I choose to love myself fully and without conditions.

28

JANUARY

MAKE A COLLAGE OF YOUR LIFE

Create a beautiful collage that reflects your life. Use images, words, pictures, and phrases from magazines or websites to make something beautiful that represents what is meaningful to you. This collage can serve as a reminder that all of life's various pieces assembled together can be made into something uniquely special!

29

JANUARY

FOCUS ON THE WHOLE, NOT THE HOLE

Imagine a donut in front of you. Do you focus on the whole donut or the hole in the middle? This donut represents what you have in your life. Pay more attention to the good in your life rather than what's missing.

30
JANUARY

GIVE YOURSELF A HUG

Try to stop your negative self-talk by just giving yourself a hug. Throughout the day, when you feel like you need soothing, hug yourself as you express loving thoughts. We all need hugs, and most of us don't hesitate giving them to our loved ones. Why wouldn't you be as worthy as your inner circle?

31

REFRAME COGNITIVE DISTORTIONS

Cognitive distortions are unhealthy thinking habits that can cause low self-esteem. Here are some examples:

All-or-nothing thinking: "No one likes me."
Healthier thought: "I have trouble connecting with others."

Fortune-telling: "I'll never get my life together."
Healthier thought: "I feel discouraged right now."

Labeling: "I'm an idiot."
Healthier thought: "I sometimes make mistakes, just like everybody else."

Now it's your turn! Try to identify your cognitive distortions and replace them with healthier thoughts throughout your day.

FEBRUARY

1

VISUALIZE ACCEPTANCE

Self-esteem suffers when self-acceptance is low, but practicing acceptance helps stop rumination and self-doubt. Imagine you are on a bridge with a train passing underneath. Each boxcar is a negative memory or thought pertaining to the past. Using what's called an "observing head," watch the train go by instead of reacting to it. From a distance, observe those painful memories in a detached way. Try to look *at* those thoughts rather than *from* those thoughts.

2

FEBRUARY

INSTEAD OF BEING RIGHT, BE KIND

In relationships with others, always choose being kind over being right. Arguments happen when people try to prove how right they are.

3

FROM VICTIM TO VICTOR

Refusing to adopt a victim mentality is a major step toward self-care. Instead, choose to think in *victorious* ways that put you in control of your feelings and thoughts. Changing your "victim" language into "victor" language does wonders for self-esteem. For example, replace "He made me mad" with "I was mad when he said that." Think of examples in your own life where you can change victim language into victor language.

4

FEBRUARY

WHAT MAKES YOU UNIQUE?

Think about a quality you have that truly makes you YOU. What positive things has it brought to your life?

5

REPLACE CRITICISMS WITH ENCOURAGEMENT

Today, focus on replacing any negative or critical thought about yourself with a positive one. For example, if you think "I shouldn't have said that," replace that negative thought with something more positive, like "Good for you for trying to speak up." Choose encouragement over criticism every time.

6

FEBRUARY

YOU ARE IMPORTANT

If you could only sense how important you are to the lives of those you meet.

—FRED ROGERS (MR. ROGERS)

7

STOP SIGN

When your self-esteem feels low, chances are you are succumbing to negative thoughts. When that happens, imagine a STOP sign. This will remind you to stop the negative thoughts that shake your confidence. Replace them with more positive thoughts based on fact. For more impact, say "STOP" out loud, even if it is just quietly to yourself. Then imagine a green stoplight for GO when you replace negative thoughts with more positive thoughts.

8

FEBRUARY

OUT WITH BITTERNESS, IN WITH ACCEPTANCE

Replace bitterness with acceptance, and everything else will fall into place.

9

FEBRUARY

COMMUNICATE ASSERTIVELY

Nonassertive communication and low self-esteem go hand in hand. Rather than worrying about what others think, focus on using "I" statements today. Start with statements like "I think" or "I feel" and be descriptive. "You" statements are aggressive, controlling, and place blame on others. "I" statements are assertive and show respect to yourself and others. For example:

"You" statement: "You interrupted me again."

"I" statement: "I would like to finish what I was saying."

10

FEBRUARY

DON'T LIVE IN THE REARVIEW MIRROR

Nothing diminishes self-esteem more than living life looking backward, as if in the rearview mirror, reworking yesterday. Today, make an effort to live life moving forward with optimism and hope.

11

FEBRUARY

LOVE YOURSELF AND YOUR LIFE

Loving yourself and loving your life go hand in hand. What messages do you tell yourself that rob you of self-love? Write them down on one side of a note card, then counter them with loving messages on the other side. For example, you could replace "I am too sensitive" with "I care very deeply about things." When you work on being kinder to yourself, you will love yourself—and your life—more!

12

FEBRUARY

DON'T LOSE YOURSELF

In unhealthy relationships, personal growth is sacrificed. Never lose yourself trying to find someone else. Choose your relationships wisely—only let in people who are good for your self-esteem!

13

YOU CAN'T UNDO THE PAST

Let's remember: Don't try to saw sawdust.

—DALE CARNEGIE

14

FEBRUARY

WHAT'S YOUR MANTRA?

Personal mantras can help guide us and nurture us when we feel stressed and find ourselves lacking confidence. Think of a personal mantra you can repeat to keep you centered and confident, like "I can get through this" or "I am getting stronger every day."

15

FEBRUARY

JOURNAL TOWARD HEALING

If you can't seem to get over hurts from the past, you will feel like a victim. Use your journal to help you heal, reflecting on the following ideas:

- Write down some hurts from the past, expressing and acknowledging them.
- How have you grown from your regrets? What lessons have you learned?
- How have these experiences helped you gain empathy for others?
- What do you need to heal moving forward? Make an action plan, even with small baby steps.

16

FEBRUARY

CHOOSE TO BE MINDFUL

When you practice mindfulness—staying aware in the moment—you suspend judgment of how things "should" be and become more accepting of what actually is.

17

PHYSICAL SELF-CARE

Taking time to nurture your physical health will help your overall self-esteem. What habits for physical well-being would you like to incorporate into your life? Do you try to be physically active? Do you make an effort to eat nutritious food? Do you have checkups with your doctor? Write down goals to improve your physical well-being. Keep a calendar, journal, or checklist that can help you stick to those goals.

18

FEBRUARY

YOU ARE RESPONSIBLE FOR YOUR HAPPINESS

Part of healing from past hurts and improving self-esteem is looking for your happiness within yourself. You can't change what happened to you, but you can choose your response.

19
FEBRUARY

AN AFFIRMATION FOR SETTING LIMITS

I will say no if I need to. Setting limits is an act of self-love.

20
FEBRUARY

YOU DON'T HAVE TO GO TOO FAR

Sometimes just one step in another direction can change your life. Think of one step in a positive direction you can make today.

21

CULTIVATE LOVING-KINDNESS

When we are hard on ourselves, our self-esteem takes a back seat. Think of ways to cultivate loving-kindness toward yourself. It can be as simple as savoring a cup of tea, looking in the mirror and saying something kind to yourself, writing a love note to yourself, or writing down what you admire about yourself. Practice at least one action today to get closer to loving self-kindness.

22

FEBRUARY

WEAKEN OR DEEPEN

After a setback, loss, or trauma, we either weaken or deepen. When we weaken, we become a victim of circumstance. When we deepen, we get stronger and more resilient from overcoming obstacles. Which one will you choose?

23

THOUGHTS ON A CLOUD

Imagine putting your unhealthy and unwanted thoughts on a cloud. Watch them disappear. Do not try to alter their pace as they float by. Just observe those clouds that contain your unwanted thoughts with nonjudgmental awareness, allowing some distance between them and you.

24

FEBRUARY

BE WILLING TO LEAVE THINGS BEHIND

Sometimes we need to leave things behind so that we can move toward something else that fits us better in the moment.

25

AN AFFIRMATION FOR MOVING FORWARD

I refuse to give the past more power than the present.

26

FEBRUARY

UNHEALTHY MINDSETS

Some people may not be able to give you what they don't have to give. Forgive them for not being as healthy as you had hoped, and move forward. After all, you don't expect to buy fruit at a hardware store.

27

CHANGE JUDGMENTS INTO QUESTIONS

Identify how you talk to yourself and determine whether it is judgmental or not. Chances are, if your self-esteem is taking a hit, you are likely not talking kindly to yourself. Turn your critical thoughts into questions. Questions show hope, flexibility, and a growth mindset. For example, "I can't seem to get my life together" can be replaced with "What do I need to do to get the life that I want?"

28

FEBRUARY

WELCOME STRESS IN YOUR LIFE

Empower yourself by welcoming stress in your life. Think about challenges in your life that have led to growth.

29

IMPORTANT QUESTIONS

Consider the following questions at the end of every day to help you stay true to yourself.

Did I make the day count?

Did I stand up for what I believe in, even if I felt alone?

Did I show and express love?

Did I hold true to my values?

Reflect on these questions as a daily practice and write about them in your journal. This will help you review your growth and progress.

MARCH

1

VOLUNTEER AND GET INVOLVED

How can you use your talents to help others? When we focus on something greater than ourselves, our self-esteem also gets a boost. Are you good at organizing or making flyers? Are you especially good with animals? Maybe you've always wanted to try coaching. Choose something you might be interested in and volunteer for it. You have so much to offer!

2

MARCH

AN AFFIRMATION FOR TAKING IT EASY

I will stop being so hard on myself. I don't deserve to beat myself up for things I did when I did not know better.

3

DON'T JUST HEAR, LISTEN

When we listen—and not just hear—our relationships benefit. Hearing involves reacting to just the audible words, while listening is more active—empathizing, summarizing, and supporting. For example, let's say a friend tells you she is dreading a family visit. When you're just *hearing* her, you'd say, "Don't worry about it—it will be fine." But active listening would look like "I can see you are really anxious about the visit—it's tough being uncertain of how things will go." How can you use active listening today?

4

YESTERDAY IS DONE

Finish every day and be done with it. You have done what you could.

—RALPH WALDO EMERSON

5
MARCH

MEASURE UP TO YOURSELF

Never measure yourself by someone else's yardstick—you might never measure up to their expectations. Trust your own standards.

6
MARCH

FILL YOUR BUCKET

Imagine carrying around an imaginary bucket that is full of the messages you give yourself. Do you carry around messages that are critical or supportive? Today, write only supportive, kind thoughts about yourself, including some of your positive attributes. Write them down or print them out, and cut each idea into strips to put in a physical bucket or container. Refer to these positive messages often, especially on days when you doubt yourself and your greatness.

7

MARCH

APPRECIATE TODAY

Commit to appreciating this day, no matter what. You may find that you'd give anything to have it back.

8

MARCH

FOCUS ON YOUR STRENGTHS

Instead of taking an inventory of your shortcomings, focus on taking an inventory of your strengths. What are you proud of about yourself? What strengths do you have that have helped you make meaningful contributions to your world? What attributes do you have that you are the most proud of? Write your answers down in a journal or notebook and refer to them when you need a self-esteem boost.

9

MARCH

AN AFFIRMATION FOR SMALL STEPS

Small steps in my life help me make big changes.

10

MARCH

KEEP MOVING FORWARD

No matter how old you are, how tired you are, or how discouraged you might be, it's never too late to build on yesterday and keep moving forward.

11

WAIT!

Take inventory of your negative thoughts by using the acronym WAIT, which offers two questions that will help you defeat thoughts that pull you down: "What Am I Thinking?" and "What Are Irrational Thoughts?" Practice WAITing by following the below example:

Irrational Thought: "He made me so mad yesterday. I can't stand him."

Rational Alternative: "I was mad when he raised his voice to me. I will let him know I found it disrespectful."

What irrational thoughts can you reframe today?

12
MARCH

SECOND CHANCES

If you find yourself held back by regrets and mistakes, focus on the lessons learned instead. There are no do-overs, but there are second chances.

13
MARCH

BEAUTIFUL AS A RAINBOW

We don't judge the rainbow, thinking there should be more blue or a little less yellow. It's beautiful the way it is, and so are you.

14

START THE DAY WITH A POSITIVE INTENTION

When you think positively, you feel more positive. This morning, choose a positive intention, such as "Today I will look for the good in everyone and treat others with kindness." Remind yourself of this intention throughout the day. Consider making a daily habit of starting each day with a new positive intention.

15

MARCH

DON'T FOCUS ON WASTED TIME

When stuck in feelings of regret, remember that the more you focus on time wasted, the more you waste time being a prisoner of your past.

16

MARCH

TAKE COMPLIMENTS WITH CONFIDENCE

If your self-esteem is low, chances are you have trouble accepting compliments. You might think you don't deserve them or don't want to seem full of yourself. Instead of being modest, a simple "thank you" or "I appreciate that" is a good way to accept compliments assertively. Today, give yourself some compliments and practice accepting them with confidence.

17

MARCH

LOVE YOURSELF

The true foundation for any healthy relationship is your ability to love yourself. The more you value yourself, the more you can love others without conditions.

18
MARCH

LEARN FROM YOUR FAILURES

When you have a growth mindset, mistakes and failures are your teachers, not your enemies and attackers. Write a letter to yourself using examples of how your mistakes and failures have taught you important lessons. Review the letter when you feel low and need a reminder about your resilience, and to remember what helped shape you.

19
MARCH

AN AFFIRMATION FOR WORTHY FEELINGS

I will focus on acknowledging my feelings without judging them; they are all worthy of my respect.

20
MARCH

IT'S NEVER TOO LATE

It doesn't matter what happened before. A new day is dawning, and it is never too late to make your life more beautiful.

21
MARCH

CREATE A CARING CIRCLE

Social connectedness is important for mental health and is a crucial element of a complete and balanced life. Are you connected to people who validate and support your growth? Make a list of people that you can include to expand and strengthen your circle of caring, and take practical steps to connect with each one.

22

MARCH

CHANGE YOUR MIND, CHANGE YOUR LIFE

Your old ways of thinking about problems will not bring new solutions. Choose to be solution-focused instead of problem-focused and give yourself a new perspective on old issues.

23

MARCH

GAIN YOUR OWN APPROVAL

A man cannot be comfortable without his own approval.

—MARK TWAIN

24
MARCH

RESPECT YOURSELF

One of the basic building blocks of self-esteem is self-respect. Think of ways you have shown yourself respect this week and how you can show yourself respect today. You might say no to a request, take time out for your self-care routine, identify your values, or give yourself the gift of time by not rushing. What are some other ways you can show yourself respect that you can implement in your day?

25
MARCH

SET LIMITS

Sometimes we need to say *no* to things that allow us to say *yes* to ourselves. Keep in mind that setting limits is an act of emotional survival. What can you say no to today so that you can say yes to yourself?

26

MARCH

WORDS OF COMFORT

If you find your self-esteem start to dip, look at yourself in the mirror and offer words of comfort. Speak kindly to yourself and remember that you are just as worthy as anyone else. Say words of support that you would say to someone you really value, such as "I'm proud of you," "You are a beautiful person," and "I love you."

27

MARCH

LOVE IS A GIFT

When you think of your loved ones, especially if you have children, remember that nothing you teach them is more important than the love that you give.

28
MARCH

USE YOUR SENSE OF HUMOR

Being able to laugh at life's imperfections—and your own—will help you boost self-esteem. Think of ways to add more humor in your life. Watch a silly YouTube video, watch a marathon of your favorite sitcom, or read a funny book. Try looking on the humorous side of the serious issues in your own life. A sense of humor will help you become more resilient to stress.

29
MARCH

SAVOR THE MOMENT

Don't rush today. Wherever you are, you are in the right place, at the right time, and can choose to savor the moment.

30

MARCH

TRADE IN YOUR "IF ONLYS"

Some of the most poignant statements I hear my clients say start out with
"If only . . ." Being consumed by the past leads to sadness and self-recrimination.
Try looking at it differently. For example, replace "If only I hadn't taken that
job—my life would have turned out better" with "Only if I look for another job
will I get out of the job I don't like." Give up your self-doubt by changing your
"if onlys" to "only ifs."

31

MARCH

NEVER TOO LATE

It's never too late to begin again, learn something new, and create for yourself
a happy ending.

APRIL

1

APRIL

WHAT HAVE YOU LEARNED?

An important component of self-esteem is turning both negative and positive situations into learning experiences. What have you learned recently from your past that has helped you in the present?

2

APRIL

STRESS VISUALIZATION

Stress is all about balance. Imagine stretching a rubber band. Stretch it as far as you can until it is close to snapping. Then let the rubber band go limp, which shows a lack of engagement. Now, give it some tension, which represents engagement, meaning, and growth. Strive to be motivated by stress, not debilitated by it.

3

APRIL

WRITTEN REMINDERS

When you're already feeling low, it's easy to take things personally. Try using written reminders to focus on healthier thinking. Write out personal mantras that remind you of your worth, such as "I am a good person," and "I have a right to set limits." Write them on sticky notes or note cards and put them on your computer or refrigerator or in your wallet to stay calm and grounded when you need a boost of self-esteem.

4

APRIL

COUNT FLOWERS, NOT WEEDS

Your garden will still have beautiful flowers even if there are weeds. Choose to welcome life's gifts for you, despite the inevitable weeds that arise.

5

APRIL

SLOW DOWN

Take time today to slow down. Give yourself plenty of time so you're not rushed in your daily commitments and activities. Stop racing against the clock. Take deep breaths throughout the day as you focus on staying calm and centered.

6

APRIL

SELF-LOVE IS A GIFT YOU GIVE YOURSELF

Self-love is the greatest gift you can give to yourself. After all, how can you feel good about yourself if you don't truly love yourself?

7

IDENTIFY YOUR RIGHTS

When we have low self-esteem, we are unsure of our basic human rights and may question them. Identify some of your rights, using these examples as a springboard:

I have a right to my feelings.

I have a right to express my opinion.

I have a right to not be perfect.

I have a right to set boundaries and say no.

What are some other personal rights that you value?

8
APRIL

PERSONAL LESSONS

Forgiving someone doesn't mean hanging around for more if you haven't been treated respectfully. Some people serve you better as lessons rather than people to keep in your life.

9
APRIL

GET RID OF THE ANTS

ANTs stands for *automatic negative thoughts*, which attack your self-esteem by infesting you with negative thought interpretations. For example, an ANT might be "People don't like me," when the truth is more like "I have trouble making connections." Challenge your ANTs today by writing them down in a notebook or journal and then replacing them with healthier thoughts. Time to rid yourself of those ANTS once and for all!

10

APRIL

UNPLUG TO RECHARGE

Take some time out today to unplug from your devices. Sometimes we need to unplug in order to recharge ourselves!

11

APRIL

SELF-ESTEEM MATTERS

Self-esteem isn't everything; it's just that there's nothing without it.

—GLORIA STEINEM

12

APRIL

FOCUS ON LEARNING

Some things are learned the hard way. But at least you learned something! Feeling encouraged by growing and learning is an important part of self-esteem.

13

APRIL

CHOOSE GRATITUDE

Do you let bitterness, envy, or negativity get in the way of your happiness? Instead, focus on what you are grateful for. For every negative thought that comes into your mind today, think of something you are grateful for instead. Start a list and create a gratitude practice by adding new examples to it every day.

14

COPE WITH COPING CARDS

When you are facing confidence-shaking situations, consider using coping cards. They can be physical 3 x 5 cards or digital notes on your smartphone or in your journal. Have these cards handy in times of stress. Coping cards can include:

- Affirmations
- Inspirational quotes
- Positive sayings
- Reminders
- Healthy thoughts

Draw up some coping cards today and keep them with you as needed.

15

"DON'T WORRY ABOUT IT" DOESN'T HELP

"Don't worry about it" is not a helpful statement. Positive thinking doesn't mean denying negative things; it means facing reality. Don't deny your feelings—trust your resiliency.

16

APRIL

INVEST IN YOURSELF

Invest in yourself by taking stock of your worth. We often focus on what we lack, but what about qualities you are proud of? Think of the things that are special about you. Write them down on a sticky note or in a notes app on your phone, and keep them handy in times of self-doubt. Some examples could be "I value my insight and perceptiveness" or "I am proud of how I have overcome challenges with determination and courage." Continue to add to them throughout the month.

17
APRIL

MAKE UP YOUR MIND TO BE HAPPY

Folks are usually about as happy as they make their minds up to be.

—ATTRIBUTED TO ABRAHAM LINCOLN

18

HOW YOU TALK TO YOURSELF MATTERS

Pay attention to how you talk to yourself today. Do you use comforting, kind words when you need support, or do you tend to be judgmental and negative? Talk to yourself with gentleness and respect—you deserve it!

19

MINDFULNESS FOR POSITIVITY

Mindfulness is a great tool to increase positivity and self-esteem. Give yourself a few moments of peace while lighting a candle in a dark room, watching the light flicker as you breathe slowly and deeply. No matter how dark things are in our lives, there is always light and hope. Reflect on how you can focus on light and positivity instead of the darkness around you.

20
APRIL

AN AFFIRMATION FOR ACCEPTANCCE

I have a right to my feelings, thoughts, and needs without judging or critiquing them.

21
APRIL

FEELING GOOD

What makes you feel good about yourself? In a notebook or in a notes app on your phone, write down at least five answers to that question. Look to see if any answers rely on others for approval, as in "When someone gives me a compliment." An answer like "When I feel proud of the effort I am putting into my work" is more self-empowering. The more you look to yourself for self-esteem, the more lasting it will be.

22

APRIL

LEARN FROM OTHERS

Think of people who have been special to you. Take a few moments to feel gratitude to those who have inspired you and helped you learn to take care of yourself.

23

APRIL

AN AFFIRMATION FOR YOUR YOUNGER SELF

I know I have not always been your greatest champion, but I am through revisiting regrettable moments. I am here to lift you up, not put you down.

24
APRIL

EMBRACE WHAT'S BROKEN

There are times to fix what is not working in your life, and there are times to just embrace it all—even your broken pieces. After all, mosaics are beautiful.

25
APRIL

TRANSFORM FAILURES INTO GOALS

We feel good about ourselves when we focus on growth and learning rather than when we focus on our mistakes and failures. Turning our missteps into goals ensures positive self-esteem. For example: "I failed at finding a life partner" could be "I am still looking for someone who is a good fit for a life partner." What regrets or "failures" can you turn into goals?

26
APRIL

LIVE IN THE PRESENT

Choose to ignore your ruminations about the past and worries about the future. Instead, focus on living more openly in the present.

27
APRIL

TRY A NEW ACTIVITY

Physical activity is a great stress reliever, and it boosts endorphins that can help with self-esteem. How about trying a new physical activity? For example, look up some YouTube videos on various yoga or stretching exercises, or try an app for inexperienced runners. Dance to a favorite song or take a walk in nature. Pick one new physical activity and try it out today.

28
APRIL

DON'T LET YOUR THOUGHTS CONTROL YOU

You can't control all of your thoughts, but you can make sure your thoughts are not controlling you. Remember, you are in charge.

29
APRIL

ASSERT YOURSELF

One of the best ways to increase self-esteem is to develop assertive skills. When you are assertive, you express yourself honestly and directly without fear of what people think. Identify your rights, such as "I have a right to let others know if I am upset" and "I have a right to express my feelings." Of course, you also have a responsibility to allow those same rights for others.

30

GRATITUDE HELPS YOU FORGIVE

To build on yesterday's gratitude practice, reflect on how forgiveness allows gratitude to flourish. Forgiveness does not condone bad behavior; it takes away power from those who don't deserve that trust.

MAY

1
MAY

REFLECT ON WHAT YOU'VE LEARNED

Today, take some time to reflect on what you have learned so far from this book and your responses to the reflections and practices. If you started a Self-Esteem Journal (January 10, page 6), look at some of your entries and pick the ones that are most meaningful to you. How have you grown even in just a few months?

2
MAY

LOVING OPPORTUNITIES

When you love yourself, there is nothing you can't accomplish.

3

TEMPORARY VS. PERMANENT THINKING

One of the greatest obstacles to our self-confidence is not being able to distinguish temporary from permanent thinking. Make an effort to differentiate between the two. Challenge permanent thoughts like "I am not an interesting person" with a more temporary explanation, such as "I am not confident right now, but I am taking steps to feel stronger." What examples can you think of to change your thinking from permanent to temporary?

4

NEGATIVE THOUGHTS ARE LIKE WEEDS

Do not allow negative thoughts to enter your mind for they are the weeds that strangle confidence.

—BRUCE LEE

5
MAY

MAKE THE BEST OF EVERYTHING

Instead of waiting for things to turn out for the best, try to make the best of everything.

6
MAY

DIFFERENTIATE SHAME FROM GUILT

Although *shame* and *guilt* are often confused, shame is damaging to self-esteem, while guilt can be productive and healthy. We can learn from our regrets, make amends, and improve our behavior. Shame, on the other hand, is not about *doing* something bad—it is about *viewing yourself as bad*. Shame damages self-esteem, while guilt, within limits, can help us be better. Write down some examples of shame and guilt from your life to learn the difference.

7
MAY

BE YOUR OWN BEST FRIEND

When you are too hard on yourself, think of how you would talk to a best friend. Would you be kind and caring? Be your own best friend and speak kindly to yourself.

8
MAY

MINDFULNESS PRACTICE

A mindful practice is an act of present-centered, nonjudgmental awareness. You can use it in everything you do, even getting dressed, washing dishes, or working. Mindfulness helps you heal from the past because it focuses on the present moment. Try to be mindful in everything you do. Catch judgments like "I can't stand dirty dishes in the sink" and try to accept things as they are.

9
MAY

FROM ANGER TO DANGER

Lessons taught with love are learned much better than lessons taught in anger. Those lessons end up backfiring, derailing confidence in yourself and in others. Remember, *anger* is one letter short of *danger*!

10
MAY

GET INSPIRED!

Inspirational quotes help us stay grounded and positive, and will help you on your journey to self-confidence and self-love. Find various quotes online that inspire you and help boost your confidence and optimism, and print each of them out on its own page. Put them in a picture frame or plexiglass sign holder, rotating them daily. You can even write some of your own, too!

11
MAY

BE KIND TO YOURSELF

Learning to be kind to yourself is one of the greatest gifts you can give to yourself. Try it today!

12
MAY

AN AFFIRMATION FOR MY ATTITUDE

The only thing between an *okay* day and an *amazing* day is my attitude.

13
MAY

MAKE A SELF-CARE PLAN

Make a list of actions you can take to practice self-care, and create a self-care plan for the month. Some examples might be:

- Committing to a regular exercise routine (be specific)
- Keeping a journal to write down your thoughts and feelings
- Setting aside 15 minutes a day to read self-help/inspirational passages
- Starting the day with a positive affirmation or intention
- Practicing yoga or mindfulness

Use these examples as a springboard to devise a self-care plan you can follow, making daily notes for each item to track your progress.

14
MAY

YOU NEED YOURSELF MORE

If you find yourself with someone who can't accept you for who you are, let them go. You need yourself much more.

15
MAY

HELPFUL TOUCHSTONES

Using a touchstone can help you stay grounded when your self-esteem starts to slip. A touchstone is an actual object that helps calm and ground us in times of stress. It can be a polished gem, a comforting photo, a quote or affirmation, or any metaphorical object that reminds you of your worth. You can keep a touchstone in your purse or pocket to provide comfort when you need a self-esteem boost.

16

YOU ARE IN CONTROL

You may not control all the events that happen to you, but you can decide not to be reduced by them.

—MAYA ANGELOU

17
MAY

BE AUTHENTIC, NOT PERFECT

Perfection derails self-esteem and self-confidence by setting unrealistic expectations for ourselves. Instead, strive to be authentic rather than perfect. Reflect on how your life would be different if you focused on being more authentic.

18
MAY

TAKE A SELF-COMPASSION BREAK

When you're feeling critical toward yourself, give yourself a self-compassion break with this simple practice: Put your hand on your heart and massage it, or anywhere else on your body you find soothing, and say comforting words to yourself, such as "I am a beautiful person," "May I treat myself with kindness," or "May I love myself the way I deserve."

19
MAY

CELEBRATE YOU!

Consider the beautiful person that you are and celebrate yourself today. Smile, be silly, laugh, and find the good in everything around you.

20
MAY

SELF-COMPASSION LETTER

What do you know now that you did not know when you were younger? Write a letter of forgiveness to your younger self for learning things a little later than you would have liked. If you have regrets, show your younger self empathy rather than criticism. Your younger self deserves lots of love—as you do now.

21
MAY

MOVE FROM TRAUMA TO GROWTH

Post-traumatic stress defines us by our past, whereas post-traumatic growth focuses on moving past the trauma with scars and lessons learned, making us wiser.

22
MAY

CHANGE YOUR LANGUAGE, CHANGE YOUR DESTINY

Tired of listening to years of old messages that erode your self-esteem? Try talking to yourself with a new perspective. For example, replace "Things would be so much better if that hadn't happened" with "I am thankful for the opportunity to build on my experience." Or replace "Why me?" with "I will move forward from these setbacks stronger." Think of how you can change your language about the past to empower you in the present.

23
MAY

CULTIVATE GRATITUDE

Focus on the roses instead of the thorns. Today, look for things that you are grateful for.

24
MAY

CHOOSE LEARNING OVER ENVY

The success of another person does not diminish your worth. Instead, see them as role models to help light your way.

25
MAY

POSSIBILITY THINKING

If you have low self-esteem, you may tend to think in terms of problems rather than possibilities. Focus on your possibilities instead. For example, a problematic thought might be "I am unhappy with my limited support system." Reframe that to something like "I look forward to joining new groups and activities, meeting new people, and expanding my support system." Now it's your turn to transform your problems into possibilities.

26
MAY

LET GO OF BITTERNESS

Once you let go of the bitterness over what you don't have in life, you can embrace with gratitude everything life does have to give.

27
MAY

REFRAME NEGATIVE SELF-TALK

Challenge your negative self-talk by reframing it into questions. This encourages you to challenge negative beliefs instead of believing them. For instance, "I can't take it anymore" could become "What do I need to do to get through this?" In the first sentence, you're surrendering your power and thinking in extreme, all-or-nothing ways. But the question allows you to look forward, with you in control. What negative thoughts can you reframe into questions today?

28
MAY

AN AFFIRMATION FOR SELF-FORGIVENESS

I forgive myself for not having the foresight to know what is now so obvious in hindsight.

29
MAY

UNCONDITIONAL SELF-LOVE

When you love yourself unconditionally—not when you are 10 pounds thinner, get a better job, or find a partner—you are more likely to find happiness.

30
MAY

EACH DAY IS A NEW BEGINNING

When the past no longer has a hold on you, you can live each day like it's a new day with infinite possibilities.

31

FORGIVENESS SETS YOU FREE FROM THE PAST

It's hard to move forward when you are unable to forgive. Luckily, there is no shortage of opportunities. Reflect on the ideas below and add to the list from your own life:

- Forgive yourself for not being "perfect."
- Forgive your imperfect parents for doing the best they could.
- Forgive life for not always going your way.
- Forgive your friends and family for slighting you.
- Forgive others for not seeing things "your way."

JUNE

1

SOCIAL SELF-CARE

Although some view self-care as an individual process, sometimes the best self-care involves being social and connecting with others for support. Do you neglect relationships because you are just too busy? Are you making time to stay connected with your friends and family? Think of at least one way to make your connections a priority and take one actionable step toward that today.

2

JUNE

DON'T GIVE UP ON YOURSELF

You may need to give up relationships that don't support your growth. Otherwise, you may be giving up on yourself.

3

TRY SOMETHING NEW

Our self-esteem thrives when we have the courage to move out of our comfort zone and try something new. What new behaviors would you like to do? What is stopping you? It might be approaching someone you would like to get to know, expressing yourself more freely to another person, starting a memoir, or trying a new hobby. Make a list of new things you would like to try and start one of them today!

4

JUNE

DON'T TRY TO CHANGE OTHERS

One major cause of relationship conflict is attempting to change other people, including trying to change their minds. The only person you can ever really change is yourself. In relationships, unconditional acceptance is the key. Love them, don't judge them.

JUNE

WRITE YOURSELF A LOVE LETTER

When we think of love letters, we often think of writing to someone else. However, the most important relationship you will ever have is with yourself; it is the cornerstone of healthy relationships with others. Spend some time reflecting on why you are lovable and write about those reasons. What are you proud of? How have you moved through difficult times with courage and sincerity? How have you turned weakness into strength?

JUNE

AN AFFIRMATION FOR HAPPINESS

I have no preconditions for my happiness. I choose happiness today no matter what.

7

JUNE

PRODUCTIVE VS. UNPRODUCTIVE REGRET

Regret can be productive if it uses lessons of the past to help us improve moving forward. How can you make your unproductive regrets productive?

8

JUNE

ALL THE WRONG PLACES

Never look for happiness in a place where you lost it to begin with.

9

JUNE

OBSERVE, DON'T JUDGE

During times of self-doubt, observe your negative thoughts rather than buying into them. For example, if you think "I am a failure," you could reframe the thought to "I am having the thought that I am a failure." When you look *at* your negative thoughts rather than operating *from* those thoughts, you're less likely to believe them. Try it out today!

10

JUNE

MELT AWAY SELF-DOUBT

Make the decision to love and accept yourself, and your self-doubt will melt away.

11

USE OPTIMISTIC LABELS

Pessimistic labels lead to passivity, whereas optimistic ones lead to attempts to change.

—MARTIN E. P. SELIGMAN

12

THE POWER OF A THOUGHT

Fill a clear glass with water. Put in one drop of food coloring and stir it around. Notice how that one drop discolors the water. Now imagine that drop as a negative thought. Just think of how many negative thoughts per day can be self-sabotaging and will muddy your perspective! Remember this visualization when you find yourself overwhelmed with negative thoughts.

13
JUNE

LEAD AN AUTHENTIC LIFE

Do you lead an authentic life, or are you living life the way you think others expect or want you to be? Trust your journey without fear of what others think.

14
JUNE

APPRECIATING OTHERS—AND YOURSELF!

For every interaction with another person today, think of one way to show them love and express appreciation. Some ideas might be paying a compliment, doing something for someone without expecting anything in return, or surprising someone with a thoughtful card, text, or voice mail that lets them know how much they mean to you. Don't forget including yourself in these acts of gratitude and loving-kindness!

15
JUNE

BE FLEXIBLE

Flexibility is the key to a resilient growth mindset. Try this exercise: Fold your arms and notice which arm is on top. Now fold your arms the other way so the other arm is on top. How does it feel? In any group situation, about half the group feels comfortable with the left arm on top, and half with the right. Everyone has different comfort zones. What can you do to keep your perspective flexible?

16
JUNE

LIGHTEN YOUR LOAD

Are you carrying around too much emotional baggage from yesterday? Lighten your load by staying focused on the present and practicing mindful awareness.

17

GET GOING TODAY!

Physical activity increases self-esteem. Find ways to incorporate more exercise into your life. Park at the end of the parking lot so you can increase your steps. Walk around the block one extra time, or take the steps instead of the elevator. If you are watching TV, do some mat exercises while you watch. Get motivated to get going!

18

JUNE

SURROUND YOURSELF WITH SUPPORT

The quality of our support system leads directly to the quality of our lives. Do your most important connections build you up or tear you down?

19

JUNE

IDENTIFY YOUR CORE BELIEFS

Self-doubt is rooted in negative core beliefs that distort reality. To discover your core beliefs, follow these steps:

1. Write down a negative self-statement, such as "I have nothing to say in meetings."

2. Ask yourself what it would mean if that statement was true. (e.g., "I would hate if they thought I wasn't smart.")

3. Ask yourself what it would mean if your second statement was true. (e.g., "It would mean I am not smart.")

When you dig deep to the core by questioning your erroneous beliefs, you will realize how false your core belief is. You can then counter with a more rational thought, such as "What I have to say in meetings is just as important as everyone else."

20

JUNE

SEE THE GLASS HALF FULL

We can choose to see the glass half full or half empty. Choose a life narrative that builds you up rather than tears you down.

21

JUNE

CHOOSE SELF-COMPASSION

Self-compassion is simply giving the same kindness to ourselves that we would give to others.

—CHRISTOPHER GERMER

22
JUNE

TREAT YOURSELF

How can you treat yourself today? Think of yourself as a good friend who deserves special treatment. Could you buy yourself a present, give yourself more time to relax and refresh, spend extra time with a hot cup of tea or coffee and savor every sip, or call an old friend or family member to catch up? When we are good to ourselves, we feel better about ourselves—and our lives.

23
JUNE

DON'T RUN ON EMPTY

If you feel depleted, what can you do to take care of yourself? You can't truly give to others if you are running on empty.

24
JUNE

AN AFFIRMATION FOR HOPE

When I feel discouraged, I look for glimmers of hope. The rainbow never comes without the rain.

25
JUNE

THINK OF SOMEONE SPECIAL

Reflect on people whose care for you has made a big impact on your life. Treasuring your meaningful connections can help you feel more positive.

26
JUNE

YOUR LIFE IS RICH IN MEANING

Even when it is not easy, your dedication and perseverance to move forward despite challenges makes your life rich in meaning.

27
JUNE

LEAVES IN A STREAM

Practice the habit of mentally noting any self-sabotaging thoughts and feelings instead of reacting to them. Visualize your negative thoughts or feelings like they are on leaves in a stream. Watch them slowly move with the current, away from you. Detach yourself from those negative thoughts while they float into the distance and disperse. This practice is very helpful in improving self-esteem, as it roots you in the present with mindful awareness.

28

JUNE

ALLOW ROOM FOR ERROR

Fresh starts don't always work out as planned; the path to happiness and self-esteem is not linear. You may need to welcome some missteps among many fresh starts. Missteps are all part of an authentic life journey.

29

JUNE

MAKE SMALL STEPS

Small steps in your life can help you make big changes in your self-esteem. Don't underestimate the importance of little decisions you make each day and small actions that help you make yourself a priority. Saying no to a request, doing a daily mindful practice, and writing in your journal are all small steps toward your goal of choosing to love yourself. Write down five ways you can take small steps this week.

30

USING YOUR SENSES

Mindful awareness helps alleviate stress and clear your thinking. Right now, focus on the present sensation of your senses. Spend a few minutes noticing what you hear, feel, taste, smell, and see. Keep a running list by writing down at least three examples of each of your five senses each time. Write your answers in a journal if you keep one, or consider starting a separate mindfulness journal to keep track of your sensations.

JULY

1

JULY

DON'T WAIT

You are just as worthy along the journey as you are when you arrive at your destination. Don't wait until life comes together to love and accept yourself.

2

JULY

SPIRITUAL SELF-CARE

Practicing spiritual self-care can help replenish your soul. You might read a devotional or something inspirational each morning, or try yoga, meditation, prayer, or journaling. You can attend to your spirituality by connecting with nature or connecting with others as part of a spiritual community. There are many ways to incorporate spiritual self-care that help you feel part of something greater than yourself.

3
JULY

FREEDOM FROM YOUR "MONKEY MIND"

Become independent of your "monkey mind," which is the unsettled chatter in your head telling yourself that you aren't good enough. Instead, only listen if your internal voice is loving and accepting.

4
JULY

YOU DESERVE SELF-RESPECT

How can you demonstrate more self-respect? Set better boundaries, stand up for yourself, or take more time to relax? Self-respect is necessary for true self-esteem.

5

JULY

"STRESSED" SPELLED BACKWARD IS "DESSERTS"

Stress is inevitable, but it's probably no coincidence that "stressed" spelled backward is "desserts." Stress can be sweet if you manage it instead of letting it overwhelm you. We need stress in our lives to truly grow.

6

JULY

APPRECIATE YOURSELF

We have all heard of the various appreciation days people celebrate, such as Teacher Appreciation Day, or Daughter or Son Appreciation Day. How about a *YOU* Appreciation Day? This is the day to honor yourself and pay yourself special attention! Take yourself out on a date, buy something you've been wanting, or treat yourself to a spa visit, massage, or special movie and snack. Whatever makes you feel special, do it!

7

A DAILY REMINDER

Every day brings a chance for you to draw in a breath, kick off your shoes, and step out and dance.

—OPRAH WINFREY

8

JULY

COMPASSIONATE CHECKLIST

Keep a journal (page 6) to personalize your self-compassion journey. Let this checklist be your guide to unconditional self-love. Use the following ideas as writing prompts for your journaling:

- Be kind to yourself.
- Practice being nonjudgmental.
- Forgive yourself for everything.
- Love yourself without conditions.
- Give yourself words of encouragement.
- Accept yourself with no strings attached.

What else can you add to this list?

9
JULY

AN AFFIRMATION FOR RESILIENCE

Today I will focus not on what I lost or what went wrong in my life, but on what I have left with hope for my future.

10
JULY

TAKE CHARGE OF YOUR THOUGHTS

You can't change your feelings, but you can change the thoughts that created them. The following is an example of how to change your thoughts to change your reactions, which leads to better results. Let's say you broke up with your partner. You may think "I am never going to get over this." The consequence of that thought would be anxiety, heart palpitations, sweating, and depression. But you can change your thought to something like "It hurts, but I will grow from this to improve my relationships going forward." The new consequence would be that you're more calm and confident. Now it's your turn! What thoughts can you take charge of?

11
JULY

YOU'RE AWESOME!

Just in case you forget how awesome you are, consider this a reminder!

12
JULY

GRATITUDE MEDITATION

Spend a few minutes in a meditative state, sitting quietly and slowing down your breath, breathing from your diaphragm rather than shallow chest breathing. Breathe in through your nose and out through your mouth. No matter how difficult your road might be, be thankful for the opportunity to improve upon yesterday. Imagine gratitude cradling you as you accept where you are in your life right now as the place where you should be. Appreciate the beauty inside and outside of yourself.

13
JULY

LOOK FOR THE GOOD

Make a conscious effort to look for the good in everything you experience, in yourself and others. Then spread it around!

14
JULY

RADICAL ACCEPTANCE

Strive to accept, with complete and total acknowledgment, things that cannot be changed. This is called *radical acceptance*, and it boosts your self-esteem. Think of the things you struggle with that you can transform this way. You can do this with a few moments of contemplation and mindful meditation, writing in a journal, or even speaking kindly to yourself. Try one of these today.

15
JULY

ALL YOU HAVE ACCOMPLISHED

Think about what makes you proud about yourself and what you have accomplished. What accomplishments can help you move toward your goals?

16
JULY

BODY SCAN

Mindfulness practices boost self-esteem by helping us relax and stay calm, present, and focused so we are not consumed by anxieties. A useful mindfulness technique is the body scan. Relax, slow your breath, and close your eyes. Starting from your toes and ending with your head, bring your attention to the different parts of your body, becoming aware of every sensation. Appreciate what each part of your body does for you.

17

AVOID THE COMPARISON TRAP

Comparison with others provides a faulty measure of our self-worth. Instead, measure your own progress over where you were yesterday.

18

TRANSFORM YOUR FAILURES INTO STEPPING-STONES

Failures can undermine self-esteem, but they can also become stepping-stones to success. There are countless stories of famous people who experienced failure on the road to success—Oprah Winfrey, Michael Jordan, and Steve Jobs are just a few examples. In a journal or a notebook, write down a few failures or setbacks that you have had and write one good thing that came out of each.

19
JULY

QUELL YOUR INNER CRITIC

We often say things to ourselves we wouldn't consider saying to others. Tame your inner critic by refusing to listen to those unkind, self-sabotaging thoughts.

20
JULY

TAKE A MINDFUL MINUTE

One of the central components of self-compassion is mindfulness. Mindfulness helps us tame our negative thoughts by being aware of them without reacting to or judging them. Throughout the day, take several mindful minutes to focus on showing yourself love and acceptance. In these moments, breathe slowly and practice nonjudgmental awareness. Let your negative thoughts pass by, watching without believing them.

21
JULY

PUT YOUR MASK ON FIRST

As a flight attendant would say in an emergency, put your mask on first so you can help yourself, and then help others.

22
JULY

SEPARATING THOUGHTS FROM FEELINGS

Good self-esteem is based on the ability to separate feelings from thoughts. For example, "You left me out to dry" is a thought, not a feeling. The resulting feelings are anger and sadness. A more rational thought might be "I feel angry because I don't think you've been supportive," while still acknowledging your feelings. Try to change the thoughts that create your negative feelings. What examples can you think of in your own life?

23
JULY

YOUR SELF-WORTH IS IN YOUR CONTROL

No one can make you feel inferior without your consent.

—ELEANOR ROOSEVELT

24
JULY

YOU CAN ONLY CHANGE YOURSELF

Trying to change people is like trying to change the weather—better just to carry an umbrella!

25
JULY

EMBRACE STRESS

Our self-esteem takes a hit when we find stress hard to manage. Make a list of 10 responses to the phrase "Stress is (blank)." What do you notice? If you are like most people, you will likely describe stress as generally negative. Put a minus next to each answer that is negative, and a plus next to positive stressors. Some may be both. This practice shows us that stress can be just as positive as well as negative, and can be motivating.

26
JULY

HAPPINESS IS ALL IN YOUR ATTITUDE

Happiness does not come from the outside; it's an inside job. We can only make ourselves happy. It's all about what happens between your ears!

27

JULY

IMPROVE YOUR SELF-TALK

Negative self-talk punches holes in our self-esteem. Turn negative messages into positive ones with this practice: Get a flat-bottom coffee filter. On the outside bottom of the filter, write a negative thought about yourself. Write a positive alternative on the inside. Stand the negative side (bottom) faceup and let it go. As you watch it drop, notice that the filter always turns positive-side up as it hits the floor. Positive self-talk wins every time!

28

JULY

RELATIONSHIP SELF-CARE

Seek people who foster your growth and offer support. Set limits on your relationships that do not. Choose your inner circle carefully.

29
JULY

THE PAST ISN'T NEWSWORTHY

When we read the newspaper, we read about recent events, not old news. Imagine that you are reading old newspapers from years ago. They might be interesting to glance at, but the stories are no longer relevant. If reviewing the old news in your life brings you down, your self-esteem will suffer. How can you edit your front-page news to reflect where you are today? What is newsworthy as you move forward? Write a new front-page story that reflects who you are now.

30
JULY

AN AFFIRMATION FOR SELF-VALIDATION

Today I seek validation from only myself. I refuse to give anyone power over my self-worth.

31

MAKE A POSITIVE PLAN OF ACTION

Positive actions help you feel empowered and reduce low self-esteem. They can be visualizations, affirmations, resolutions, or intentions—anything that brings positivity to your day. Think of some you can implement right now. Some examples might be "Make an effort to smile more" or "I will set a boundary that gives me space for self-care." Consider continuing this exercise daily. Write ideas for actions down in a journal or on strips of paper to be pulled from a box.

AUGUST

1

REFLECT ON YOUR SMALL SUCCESSES

Often our small successes go unnoticed. Today, don't let that happen. At the end of the day, reflect and write down at least five things you have succeeded at. Have you expressed something that normally you would have not been confident to express? Did you show courage by setting limits on your time? Did you set aside time to declutter your workspace? Don't let your small successes go unnoticed!

2

AUGUST

WHAT DID YOU LEARN?

If you find yourself stuck in self-doubt and self-recrimination, shift from "What was I thinking?" to "What did I learn?"

3

SELF-DOUBT TIME-OUT

If self-doubt permeates your day, schedule a self-doubt time-out. Sit quietly and set one to five minutes on a timer, either once or several times per day. Use this time to indulge in your self-doubts. For the rest of the day, commit to thinking confident thoughts, waiting until the next time-out to pay attention to the negative messages you receive. This will help you get control of your self-doubts rather than letting them control you.

4

BE COMFORTABLE WITH YOURSELF

Insecurity, anxiety, and depression are incredibly common in our society, and much of this is due to self-judgment, to beating ourselves up when we feel we aren't winning in the game of life.

—KRISTIN NEFF

5

MINDFUL BREATHING

Mindfulness practices are useful in calming down the mind and body. Learning mindfulness skills can help overcome low self-esteem by slowing down repetitive, negative thinking habits that erode confidence. Mindfulness also keeps us focused on the present. Today, make an effort to slow your breathing. Focus on present thoughts and sensations rather than dwelling on past missteps and future uncertainties. Open yourself to the wonders of the present.

6

GET BETTER, NOT BITTER

When we look at what we can be thankful for rather than focus on what is missing in our lives, we become *better* rather than *bitter*.

7

AN AFFIRMATION FOR LOVING IN THE PRESENT

I accept and love myself as I am right now—without any preconditions or reservations.

8

AUGUST

ACKNOWLEDGE WEAKNESS

Allowing yourself to feel vulnerable and weak is a sign of strength. Embracing your vulnerability is a crucial factor in embracing your self-worth.

9

SELF-CARE INVENTORY

Take a self-care inventory. On a sheet of blank paper, write down the ways you take care of yourself. On the other side, write down the areas that need more care. Then, write down specific self-care goals for this week. While you're at it, try taking inventory of your internal beauty and greatness, rather than focusing on your flaws and imperfections.

10

AUGUST

DON'T LISTEN TO CRITICISM

When people remind you of where you went wrong or mistakes that you've made, you may feel worse about yourself. Remember that their negativity says more about them than you.

11

POCKET THERAPIST

Imagine you were your own therapist—what would you need to hear? What words of comfort or advice would you give yourself? Especially in times when your self-esteem is ebbing more than flowing, write out or print up self-help reminders to keep in your back pocket, wallet, or bag to keep you grounded.

12

AUGUST

SHAME WEIGHS YOU DOWN

Shame is one of the biggest self-esteem robbers. We all make mistakes, and we all have our share of failures and missteps. Don't let shame weigh you down.

13
AUGUST

LISTEN TO YOUR FAVORITE SONG

Listening to your favorite song can be a great mindfulness exercise to help calm you and boost your feelings when you are down. Find a song you love and listen to it. Take in the lyrics, harmony, voice, and instruments as if you are hearing it for the first time. What sensations and feelings does the song evoke in you?

14
AUGUST

EVALUATE YOUR DREAMS

As we move forward in life, sometimes we need to trade in our old dreams for new ones, especially if the old ones no longer serve us well.

15

AUGUST

DON'T KEEP YOUR OLD ISSUES ON LIFE SUPPORT

If you're having trouble focusing on the present when thoughts from yesterday are plaguing your mind, make an effort to be more mindful. Make a list of past regrets and challenges, and list all the ways those situations are no longer present in your life. Make a commitment to yourself now to focus on the challenges of today without reworking old issues that you are keeping on life support.

16

AUGUST

EMOTIONAL BANKRUPTCY

Focus on your emotional health like you would your financial health. Don't declare emotional bankruptcy! Make regular deposits of positive self-talk so you won't feel depleted.

17
AUGUST

THE STRESS-RESILIENT MINDSET

Research shows that just thinking about stress is bad for you, but some stressors can help us feel better about ourselves and our lives. In a notebook or journal, write down at least five ways that challenges have helped you develop a more solid foundation of self-esteem. For example, "From these challenges, I have become a more empathetic and compassionate person." Make a commitment to empower yourself in the face of stress and welcome stress as a vehicle for growth.

18
AUGUST

AN AFFIRMATION FOR ACCEPTING YOURSELF

I am a beautiful person, and I am worthy and lovable just the way I am.

19
AUGUST

BE PROACTIVE, NOT REACTIVE

Self-esteem flourishes when we are proactive and make things happen, rather than reacting to what happens. Think of possibilities instead of limitations. In your journal, write about the challenges that have pulled down your self-esteem, and about actions you can take to grow and learn from these challenges. For example, if you had an argument with your partner, practice assertive skills in the mirror, role-playing alternative ways to handle conflict.

20
AUGUST

TAKE RESPONSIBILITY, DON'T CRITICIZE

Take responsibility for your mistakes and shortcomings, but don't punish yourself for them. Critiquing does not work anywhere near as well as love and support do.

21
AUGUST

LEARN FROM FAILURE

Sometimes our biggest mistakes lay the groundwork for our greatest successes. Scotchgard was invented as a result of a spill in the 3M lab, for example!

22
AUGUST

HOW WOULD YOU DESCRIBE YOURSELF?

Think of three words or phrases to describe yourself. Do they tend to be positive or negative? Do they tend to label your perceived deficits instead of acknowledging your efforts and growth? Commit to replacing any negative statement about yourself with something more positive. For example, instead of describing yourself as "unlikable," turn that into a positive, such as "I crave to be connected and am working hard to improve my social skills."

23
AUGUST

BE YOUR OWN CHEERLEADER

Low self-esteem robs us of confidence and makes us doubt ourselves. Commit to developing self-confidence and overcoming self-doubt by cheering yourself on.

24
AUGUST

MINDFUL PRACTICES

Mindful practices can help us stay calm and confident during times of stress. They are important to our self-esteem, as they help us feel stronger. Here are some examples you can either imagine or actually do:

- Blow bubbles and watch them float away.
- Watch a pinwheel move as you blow gently.
- Imagine your anxious thoughts written on a balloon, floating away.
- Imagine your breath as a color permeating your whole body.

25

LOOK FOR REASONS, NOT EXCUSES

Excuses blame others and keep you in a state of victimhood. Reasons shed insight so you can learn from your experiences.

26

DON'T KEEP THE PAST ALIVE

Ironically, feelings and thoughts about your memories are really more about your present. These feelings keep the past alive. Commit to not allowing those thoughts to erode your sense of empowerment today. What can you learn about your feelings right now? Write your thoughts down, reflect on them, and then consider what would help you think more positively in the moment.

27

USE CALMING VISUALIZATIONS

Visualizations can be calming, soothing, and helpful in times of anxiety or distress. Imagine surrendering your stressful thoughts to the ocean and watching them disperse and disappear with each wave. Bring your attention to where you are now, and actually cup your hands and imagine yourself holding your distressing thoughts. Then separate your fingers and imagine those thoughts being released, like water slipping through your fingertips.

28
AUGUST

Forgiveness means cleansing your soul of the bitterness of "what might have been," "what should have been," and "what didn't have to happen."

—HAROLD S. KUSHNER

29
AUGUST

REFLECT ON YOUR GROWTH

How have you evolved emotionally, physically, mentally, and spiritually the past few months? Have you surprised yourself? What would you like to do more of?

30
AUGUST

IMPROVE YOURSELF

You don't need to prove yourself. Instead, seek to *improve* yourself by improving your attitude!

31

EXPRESS YOURSELF THROUGH ART

Regardless of your artistic ability, expressing yourself creatively through art can be very healing and help you feel good about yourself. Choose an idea from the list below to draw today:

- Draw how you feel today.
- Draw something important to you.
- Draw what is holding you back.
- Draw something that you learned.

Make sure you let your creative juices flow without judgment over doing things "right" or drawing perfectly.

SEPTEMBER

1

BE A MINDFUL WEATHER REPORTER

Allow yourself to observe your thoughts, sensations, and feelings as if you were a weather reporter. Even in blizzard or tornado conditions, report the weather in calm, descriptive ways, without panic or urgency. No matter how turbulent the weather is, the skies will always clear, if you are patient. Likewise, the turbulence in our minds will pass if we are patient and maintain a healthy perspective.

2

SEPTEMBER

SELF-FORGIVENESS

Forgive yourself for past stumbles and falls. Correct what you can and accept what you can't. Have the courage to try again.

3

AN AFFIRMATION FOR CHOICES

Joy, gratitude, happiness, and appreciation. Today I choose all of them.

4

SEPTEMBER

BLOSSOM IN YOUR OWN TIME

As humans, we all grow and bloom at different rates. You are allowed to blossom in your own time, at your own rate.

5

SEPTEMBER

MEDITATE ON ONE WORD OR PHRASE

Most meditation practices involve focusing on a word or phrase while breathing slowly and deeply. Choose a word or phrase that is meaningful to you, like "peace," "calm," or "I deserve to be happy." Keep focusing on that word or phrase while breathing slowly and deeply for 5 to 10 minutes. Let your thoughts come and go without getting attached to them. This practice can help you feel calm and grounded.

6

SEPTEMBER

MOVE ONWARD AND UPWARD

Keep this phrase in mind throughout your day: "Move onward and upward." It will remind you to stay positive and motivated, looking forward.

7

ATTITUDE IS A CHOICE

Your attitude is the only thing between you and an amazing life—choose a good one today!

8

SEPTEMBER

FEELINGS ARE NOT PERMANENT

Do not be fooled into thinking your feelings are permanent. Even when your self-esteem is at its lowest, keep in mind that the feelings are temporary.

9

MINDFUL DRESSING

Incorporate simple mindful practices into your everyday routine. As you dress and undress yourself today, focus on the feeling and textures of the fabric on your skin. Notice the colors and style with a fresh perspective. Our self-esteem grows when we can look at things in new ways—especially our old problems.

10

SEPTEMBER

AN AFFIRMATION FOR EMBRACING GREATNESS

Today I embrace my greatness and my strengths, and only look for the good in myself.

11

IDENTIFY YOUR "SHOULDS"

Identify the "shoulds" you say to yourself that rob you of self-esteem. Write down those "shoulds" and reframe them in a self-empowering way. For example, "I should be thinner" could be "I am developing ways to better care for my body and love myself." Refocusing each judgmental statement into an action plan will empower you and help you build confidence instead of tearing it down.

12

SEPTEMBER

DON'T HOLD ON TO OLD VERSIONS OF YOURSELF

Self-esteem suffers when we hold on to old versions of ourselves that no longer reflect who we are, and maybe that never were true anyway. Let the old versions of yourself go.

13

ENJOY NATURE

Spending time outside can be a great stress reliever and help us gain perspective. Today, spend some time enjoying nature, whether it be a walk or bike ride, or just sitting outside. While you're outdoors, repeat a positive intention or affirmation, such as "I am grateful for the beauty of nature" or "I am blessed by the beauty around me." Breathe slowly and mindfully, taking in the sights, smells, and sensations, creating meaning in this experience.

14

THE COURAGE TO BE YOU

I was once afraid of people saying, "Who does she think she is?" Now I have the courage to stand and say, "This is who I am."

—OPRAH WINFREY

15

AVOID ALL-OR-NOTHING THINKING

When you avoid all-or-nothing thinking, your self-esteem will thank you. Replace "I'm angry about everything" with "There are a lot of things that bother me." Notice how the first statement is extreme and inflexible and the second alternative is gentler and less judgmental. In a notebook or journal, write down some of your all-or-nothing thoughts that undermine confidence and transform them into self-statements that reflect a more positive growth mindset.

16

SEPTEMBER

NATURE'S SOOTHING POWER

Reflect on the soothing power and beauty of the trees, flowers, and foliage around you. Everything in nature is accepted unconditionally—don't you deserve the same?

17

OBSERVE YOURSELF IN THE THIRD PERSON

Use mindful detachment to pay attention to the present moment without judgment. This will separate your mind from negative thoughts and help calm you in times of stress. To help you detach from negative emotions and avoid overreacting, try referring to yourself in the third person: "(Your name) is watching people around them and noticing their expressions."

18

SEPTEMBER

DON'T LIVE IN THE PAST

When we are stuck in negative thoughts of the past, we give our old memories, or snapshots, too much power over our present. Those old photos are fine to look at once in a while, but you don't want to live in them!

19

FORGIVENESS HELPS YOU MOVE ON

Forgiveness is giving up all hope of a better past.

—DON FELT

20

PRACTICE BELLY BREATHING

Deep belly breathing can be calming and release stress. To start, put one hand on your stomach and take a deep breath. Watch your stomach rise as you inhale and notice how it feels. Let your thoughts go as you exhale. Let this practice bring you peace of mind today.

21
SEPTEMBER

GO FROM *WHY* TO *WHAT'S NEXT?*

Going over the "whys" of what's already transpired has limited usefulness. Try shifting to something you do have control over, like focusing on what's next.

22
SEPTEMBER

LOVE UNCONDITIONALLY

When you unconditionally love people in your life, you feel better about yourself, too. Instead of focusing on what you expect from others, consider how you can be more accepting and forgiving toward them. Nonjudgmental acceptance is one of the best gifts you can give. Anything else leads to conflict, negativity, and low self-esteem for everyone involved. What steps can you make today to fully love more and expect less? (Of course, this does not apply to abusive relationships, which are never acceptable.)

23

ANXIETY WARNING

Anxiety can provide useful information, like the gas light in a car. Heed your anxiety warnings to refill your emotional tank with self-care practices.

24

MADE WITH LOVE

Sometimes, people may have regrets in the name of love. Whether a relationship ended in a breakup, divorce, or estrangement, spending time regretting choices about things you did not know at the time wounds self-esteem to the core. Focusing on wasted time only keeps you stuck. Commit to forgiving yourself for not knowing then what you know now, and reflect on what you have learned and why you deserve forgiveness.

25

YOU CAN'T TURN BACK THE CLOCK

The more we accept that we can't turn back the clock and change our history, the more we can let go of things that cannot be changed.

26

SEPTEMBER

REMEMBER YOUR WORTH

When your self-esteem needs a boost, try this simple activity to remind you of your worth:

1. Take out a dollar bill.

2. Crease it, crumple it, fold it, and step on it (don't rip it).

3. Now smooth out the bill again.

4. Ask yourself how much the bill is worth. The answer, of course, is the same amount.

   Your worth stays the same no matter how crushed and stepped on you feel.

27

USE "GOOD ENOUGH" THINKING

Those who practice "good enough" thinking free themselves from the chains of perfectionism. How can you make peace with your perfectly imperfect self?

28

SMILE! IT'S GOOD FOR YOU

Unleash the power of a smile! Smiling consciously brightens our mood and positive feelings about ourselves. Walk around with a half-smile today—which is considered an antidote to depression—by pursing your lips slightly upward. Look in the mirror and practice. How does it look? Throughout the day, be aware of your half-smile and notice how others respond to you. Reflect on how you feel at the end of the day.

29
SEPTEMBER

BREATHE IN COLOR

Take some time for mindfulness meditation. Slow your pace and take in every-thing around you. With conscious intention, breathe slowly while imagining your breath as a color. Imagine that color going through your nose and into your extremities. As you exhale, imagine that color going out of your body through your mouth, disseminating into the air.

30
SEPTEMBER

YOU ARE BEAUTIFUL

Truly embracing your greatness is realizing that you are beautiful NOW—not when the stars align, you "prove" yourself, or when your life finally comes together.

OCTOBER

1

REFLECT ON YOUR ACCOMPLISHMENTS

Think of what you have accomplished and what you are very proud of. Have you had to overcome obstacles in your way? What did you learn about yourself by meeting these challenges? How has getting though these challenges made you stronger and more resilient?

2

OCTOBER

DECLUTTER YOUR LIFE

It is easier to be relaxed and more at peace inside our head when the space around us is less cluttered. Does your living or office area need to be stream-lined? Commit yourself to an action plan, setting aside 10 minutes a day to declutter. If you have time for more, that's great, but start with a small amount of time to clear out your space and get organized. Your mind will feel less cluttered, too!

3
OCTOBER

YOU HAVE NOTHING TO PROVE

You have nothing to prove. Work only on improving yourself, not proving yourself to others.

4
OCTOBER

HEAL YOURSELF WITH LOVE

Forgive yourself for any past actions you did out of hurt. Moving forward, trust your journey as you heal with love.

5

FRESH PERSPECTIVE

Choose to look at the world around you as if you have never seen it before. Welcoming a fresh perspective helps you develop a "beginner's mind." Take in sights, smells, sounds, and any other sensations. Look around; what do you notice that you haven't noticed before? Keep in mind the negative perceptions that taint your view currently, and reflect on what has changed and view them in a fresh light.

6

OCTOBER

CHANGE STARTS WITH YOU

If you change the way you look at things, the things you look at change.

—WAYNE DYER

7

PEOPLE BEFORE PRINCIPLES

Have any of your relationships been strained because of a disagreement or hurt feelings? What can you do today to put people before principles?

8

OCTOBER

MAKE SLEEP A PRIORITY

Sleep helps us recharge and refresh. Think of ways you can help your sleep, such as avoiding caffeine too close to bedtime or taking a bubble bath. You may incorporate a ritual, such as reading or writing in a journal or practicing a mindful meditation before bed. Make a plan to add calming practices to your self-care routine.

9

OCTOBER

TAKE STOCK OF YOUR RESILIENCE

Spend some time thinking of where you have been to get where you are now. What obstacles have you overcome? What are you most proud of?

10

OCTOBER

REPAIR BROKEN BRIDGES

Apologies go a long way in restoring relationships. It takes a lot of courage to revisit and take responsibility for your actions or words. Taking responsibility can improve your self-esteem and ability to be assertive. After all, we are human, and we all make mistakes. Is there someone you can reach out to today to make amends?

11

OCTOBER

NO ONE HAS POWER OVER YOUR BRAIN

When you think that other people upset you, remember that no one has the power to change the neurons in your brain.

12

OCTOBER

AN AFFIRMATION FOR CHANGE

I can change things about myself, accept what I can't change, and take comfort in knowing the difference.

13

HAVE A "CAN DO" ATTITUDE

Being proactive instead of reactive boosts self-esteem. Find a spare can or jar and put it somewhere to remind yourself to keep a "can do" attitude. Fill it with slips of paper with your own "can'ts" on one side and your "can do" replacements on the other. For example, replace "I can't draw" with "I can learn techniques to draw." What other examples would go in the can?

14

OCTOBER

THE IMPORTANCE OF SELF-AWARENESS

In your quest for authenticity, self-awareness is the key. Strive for insight and understanding into yourself, respecting your thoughts, feelings, and needs without judgment.

15

OWN YOUR FEELINGS

Stick to a no-blame policy today. Blaming others makes us feel powerless and gives others too much control. In the case of self-blame, it gives our past too much control. Write down ways that you blame others—or even yourself—for your feelings and change them into blameless thoughts. For example: "She hurt my feelings" would become "I was hurt when she criticized me." Own your feelings today instead of giving your power away!

16

DON'T HOLD ON TO NEGATIVITY

Your brain is like Velcro for negative experiences but Teflon for positive ones.

—RICK HANSON

17

OCTOBER

MINDFUL AWARENESS

Mindfulness practices help improve well-being by focusing on the present. Spend a few minutes focusing on today. Take time to savor moments in your day to learn something new, meet someone new, do something new, touch, smell, and taste something new. Make an effort to think in new ways that will help you love yourself and love your life.

18

OCTOBER

THE SOUL HAS NO WRINKLES

You are beautiful and valuable at any age, no matter how worn life has made you feel. Remember: The soul has no wrinkles.

19

OCTOBER

THAT ONE SPECIAL PERSON

Think about the people in your life who have helped you the most on your journey to loving yourself. Who are they? Can you identify what they have said or done that has helped you the most? Are they still in your life? If so, let them know how you feel. If not, write a letter expressing how they have mattered in your life, even if you don't send it.

20

OCTOBER

FORGIVENESS IS NOT FORGETTING

Forgiveness doesn't mean you have to forget if someone has hurt you. Forgiveness helps you heal from bitterness and negativity while still remembering the lessons so you don't go back for more.

21

OCTOBER

FORGIVE LIFE

Forgive life for not giving you everything you wanted. Sometimes not getting what you want ends up being just what you need!

22

OCTOBER

AS GOOD AS AN EGG

Visualize an uncooked egg being passed around by yourself and others in your life. Chances are the egg would be handled with extreme care so it would not break open and make a mess. Now think of how you would treat yourself—and others—differently if you used the same care in handling fragile thoughts and emotions. Don't you deserve to treat yourself—and others—as good as an egg?

23

OCTOBER

SELF-COMPASSION VISUALIZATION

To remind yourself of your worth, try this visualization practice:

1. Think of some mistakes you have made that have led to self-criticism.

2. Then, imagine that someone you admire did the same things. Would you be more empathetic?

3. Now, imagine that person fades away and becomes you.

4. With this new perspective, choose comforting words that replace self-criticism with loving self-kindness, such as "May I love myself despite my missteps."

24

OCTOBER

BE THE ARTIST OF YOUR LIFE

Your attitude is your mind's paintbrush: It paints every situation. Be the artist of your life and create a masterpiece!

25
OCTOBER

TURN COMPLAINTS INTO GOALS

One of the greatest self-esteem robbers is focusing on what is going wrong. Try to train your brain to think differently. Make a list of things you are not happy with, then write a goal for each complaint. For example, "I can't speak up at meetings because I get so nervous," can become a goal: "I will read self-help books on assertiveness and practice with a mirror to learn to speak up and express myself."

26
OCTOBER

AN AFFIRMATION FOR YOUR JOURNEY

I value the journey I am on. I appreciate the chance to live fully today and experience a brighter tomorrow.

27

MINDFULNESS HABIT

As you go through your morning rituals today—eating breakfast, taking a shower, drinking coffee, or driving your kids to school—pay particular attention to developing a habit of mindfulness. Mindfulness helps you refrain from ruminating about the past or being caught up with the "what-ifs" of the future. During your morning rituals, bring your attention to the present by opening up awareness of your five senses and noticing things you have not noticed before. Become aware of new smells, sounds, sights, sensations, and tastes. Reflect on the new awareness you gained with this mindfulness practice.

28

OCTOBER

GET BACK UP!

It does not matter how you fall or how many times you fall—what matters is how you get back up.

29

OCTOBER

VIEW YOUR PROBLEMS FROM THE OUTSIDE

Instead of looking at your problems from inside your head, get them out of your head by visualizing them as if you are viewing them on a movie screen. Imagine that you are in a movie theater and those problems are not your own; rather, they are subtitles on the big screen. You can read them, but detach yourself from them. Instead of being a character in the movie, watch from the audience!

30

OCTOBER

TREAT YOURSELF AS A DEAR FRIEND

Today and every day, treat yourself as a dear friend. This is one of the most important self-care practices you can ever do. Compliment yourself, use endearing words, smile from within, and say comforting things to yourself. When you see yourself as deserving of kindness and compassion, your self-esteem will thank you!

31

HAVE A SENSE OF HUMOR!

Remember to lighten up and look at the humor in life. Think of the times that you had that were the most fun, or when you laughed the hardest. Bring that lightness to your day today.

NOVEMBER

1

KEEP AN ATTITUDE OF GRATITUDE JOURNAL

When you choose an attitude of gratitude, acceptance and peace will be your reward. Life does not need to give you everything to be happy. Start this month off right by keeping an Attitude of Gratitude Journal. Even if you are keeping a Self-Esteem Journal (January 10, page 6), keep a separate gratitude journal this month. Write at least three new reasons why you are grateful each day. You can always write more!

2

AN AFFIRMATION TO STOP JUDGING OTHERS

I'm done with judging others. If I stop judging others, I will be less worried about if they are judging me.

3

NOVEMBER

DON'T GIVE OTHERS CONTROL OF YOUR SELF-WORTH

When we give others power over determining our worth and likability, we are no longer in control.

4

NOVEMBER

ON LOVE

Loving starts with the self.

—WAYNE DYER

5

NOVEMBER

FOCUS ON YOU

When you focus on what is special about yourself, you can replace some negative thinking patterns that erode self-esteem. Using your first or last name, describe something you like about yourself using each letter when you need a boost. For example, for the name "Mary," you could say, "Marvelous," "Adventurous," "Resilient," and "Young at heart." Can you think of more than one positive word or phrase for each letter?

6

NOVEMBER

ACCEPT YOUR PATH

Be easy on yourself when you make regrettable choices and find yourself heading in the wrong direction. Your life path does not need to be straight for it to be meaningful or successful.

7

FIVE SENSES PRACTICE

This mindfulness exercise can keep you focused on the present, limiting negative thoughts that pull down self-esteem. Slow down for a few moments and use your senses to focus on the here and now. For example:

Sound: Listen to music or sounds of nature you find soothing.

Sight: Look more closely at the beauty around you.

Smell: Breathe in fresh air or light a scented candle.

Taste: Spend a few minutes on one bite of food, savoring each sensation.

Touch: Feel the fabric of your clothes or a soft blanket.

8

NOVEMBER

—

IT'S YOUR CHOICE

Choose gratitude over bitterness. Choose forgiveness over grudges. Choose kindness over being right.

9

NOVEMBER

—

UNLEASH YOUR INNER BUTTERFLY

When you start to feel down about yourself, remember that caterpillars are stuck in their cocoons before transforming into beautiful butterflies.

10

WIN OR LOSE, YOU ARE STILL AWESOME

With a growth mindset, the goal is learning, growing, and evolving, not winning and being the best. See your losses as stepping-stones for growth. Judge yourself less and love yourself more.

11

NOVEMBER

MAKE A MOSAIC OF YOUR PAST

If your past limits your joy of today, visualize putting together the pieces of your dreams that did not materialize and make them into a beautiful mosaic. Think of an actual mosaic piece of art—the pieces that were part of something larger are broken to make something new. How can you use this visualization to turn the pieces of your life into something even more beautiful?

12

NOVEMBER

WE CAN EVOLVE IN AN INSTANT

Our evolution doesn't need to take years and years; we can grow, change, and receive flashes of insight in an instant.

13

NOVEMBER

OPEN YOURSELF UP TO NEW BEGINNINGS

Every exit leaves the door open for a brand-new grand entrance. Take a few moments to think of some of the exits you have experienced in your life and consider how they have opened up new beginnings.

14

USE REGRET TO DO BETTER

Regret doesn't remind us that we did badly. It reminds us that we know we can do better.

—KATHRYN SCHULZ

15

INSTEAD OF PROVE, IMPROVE

Instead of trying to *prove* yourself, seek to *improve* yourself. Improving shows internal growth, which boosts self-esteem. Conversely, trying to prove yourself to others—and yourself—actually diminishes self-esteem; the goal of proving yourself is based on judgment and evaluation rather than acceptance.

16

NOVEMBER

OPTIMISM IS A CHOICE

Optimism is not thinking everything turns out for the best; rather, it is thinking that YOU can still make the best out of any situation.

17
NOVEMBER

ALLOW YOURSELF TO BE VULNERABLE

Today, think of your feelings of vulnerability and consider how your vulnerability is actually a sign of courage and strength. Vulnerable feelings help open you up to growth and healing.

18
NOVEMBER

SELF-EMPOWERING THOUGHTS

If your self-esteem is taking a dip, chances are you are thinking of yourself in permanent ways, such as "I'm unlikable" or "I'm not a nice person." These descriptions are a negatively permanent way of seeing yourself. Make them more temporary: "I am having a hard time fitting in at work" or "I don't like the way I have been treating my family." Permanent ways of seeing yourself can be debilitating, but temporary thinking gives you back power.

19

CHANGE THE FRAME

Just like changing a frame to refresh the look of a picture, you can reframe your perceptions to see things in a more positive light.

1. Start by making a list of some negative thoughts, such as "I'm way too sensitive."

2. Reframe the negative thought more empathetically and positively, such as "I feel deeply about things."

3. Reflect on how it feels to reframe your critical thoughts into kinder ones.

   What critical thoughts can you reframe this week?

20
NOVEMBER

ONLY YOU CAN STRESS YOU OUT

When we learn to manage our stress, our self-esteem will grow. Ask yourself the following questions about this past week:

- Do people stress you out?
- Do people make you upset?
- Do the holidays or social gatherings stress you out?

The answer to all these questions is actually no. That is because no one and nothing can stress you out or make you feel any way. Stress is your reaction to stressful situations and people—nothing or no one can directly cause you stress. Remember, you control your thoughts and emotions. Consider how you can take charge of your stress instead of blaming others for it. You will thank yourself for it!

21
NOVEMBER

ACCEPT PEOPLE AS THEY ARE

As much as you may wish they were healthier, striving to accept others as they are will help you keep your own self-esteem intact.

22
NOVEMBER

EVALUATE YOUR LIFE BALANCE

Create a pie chart to help evaluate your current life balance. How much of your time is focused on work, family, friends, activities, spirituality, exercise, school, self-care, health, hobbies, etc.? On a piece of paper, draw a circle with a dot in the center. Next, draw a couple lines from the center, making a pie chart. Each section represents the percentage of focus you've dedicated to major areas in your life. Then create another chart representing your *ideal* life balance. Is it different? What steps can you take to make both representations more in sync?

23
NOVEMBER

CHOOSE KINDNESS EVERY TIME

When you have a choice between beating yourself up or being kind and forgiving to yourself, choose kindness every time.

24
NOVEMBER

SEE THE GOOD IN OTHERS

We feel good about ourselves when we see the good in others. Try paying one compliment to each person you interact with today. At the end of the day, reflect on how this practice made you feel.

25
NOVEMBER

GIVING THANKS

Today is a great day to focus on what you are thankful for, and also to thank others. Tell everyone you see or talk to today something about them you are thankful for. Ask them to share what *they* are thankful for.

26
NOVEMBER

AN AFFIRMATION FOR THRIVING WITH STRESS

I am not debilitated by my stress, which erodes my self-confidence. Instead, I learn from and am motivated by it.

27
NOVEMBER

EVERYDAY MOTIVATION

Start each day by reading something you find motivational—whether it be self-help books (including this one!), quotes or affirmations, or spiritual or religious passages. Find something relevant to help boost your self-esteem and deal with daily stressors. Keep a photo of your favorite quote or passage on your smartphone and refer to it often to keep a positive frame of mind.

28
NOVEMBER

TRUST YOUR JOURNEY

Just because you made a wrong turn doesn't mean it won't bring you to the right place.

29

NOVEMBER

—

OVERCOME YOUR FEARS

When our self-esteem suffers, we usually give too much power to fear and anxiety. Today, get out of your comfort zone. Choose something you are fearful of and take a chance to confront your fears instead of avoiding them. For example, if you're afraid of rejection, initiate a conversation with someone you have been wanting to meet or get to know better. Regardless of whether you are met with a welcome reception or not, if your goal is to proactively work to overcome your fears, you will achieve your goal no matter what.

30

NOVEMBER

—

REVIEW YOUR GRATITUDE JOURNAL

Did you keep an Attitude of Gratitude Journal this month (November 1, page 198)? If you did, this is a great time to review the things you were grateful for this past month. You might find that keeping a gratitude journal will help you stay positive yearlong. Positivity is one of the best self-esteem boosters.

DECEMBER

1

SIMPLE ACTS OF LOVE

This month, think of how you can spread the joy of connection and kindness to others. You might do someone a favor, text someone that you are thinking of them, or tell someone what you admire about them. The best gifts, after all, are not generally the type that you buy. When you share the nontangible gifts of love and kindness, you'll feel so much more positive and connected!

2

DECEMBER

MAKE YOURSELF A PRIORITY

Love yourself first, and everything else falls into line.

—LUCILLE BALL

3

DECEMBER

YOU DESERVE SELF-LOVE

You deserve loving words of support and encouragement as you try to take care of yourself. Do not listen to anything less than you deserve.

4

DECEMBER

STOP RENTING SPACE IN YOUR HEAD

Stop renting space in your head to the negative thoughts that rob you of your self-esteem. They are horrible tenants. Time to kick them out!

5

DECEMBER

AVOID RHETORICAL QUESTIONS

Self-esteem flourishes when we use healthy communication. Judgmental rhetorical questions will rob you of your self-esteem and distance you from others. They are really put-downs disguised as questions. Use assertive statements, such as "I'm not sure if you got my point," rather than rhetorical questions like "Didn't you pay attention?" Can you recognize other rhetorical questions you have said that end up distancing you from others in your life?

6

DECEMBER

AVOID RHETORICAL QUESTIONS TO YOURSELF, TOO

Our relationships suffer when we use rhetorical questions with others, and they are not healthy for us either. Rhetorical questions that we say to ourselves undermine our confidence. Instead of "How could I have been so dumb?" say to yourself, "I made a mistake and will learn from it." What rhetorical questions do you say to yourself? How can you rephrase them to be more kind?

7
DECEMBER

TAKE BACK YOUR POWER

No one has power over you unless you give it to them.

8
DECEMBER

SNAP OUT OF NEGATIVE THINKING

When you're feeling low about yourself, try using the rubber band technique to "snap" yourself out of your negative thoughts. Place a rubber band on your wrist, and when you identify any self-critical thoughts, snap the rubber band on your wrist to help remind you to snap out of your negative thinking. (Don't snap so hard that you hurt yourself, though. Just enough to feel it.) This is a physical reminder to challenge your self-bashing thoughts.

9
DECEMBER

WHAT IS RIGHT WITH YOU?

For everything you see wrong in yourself, think of something that is right.

10
DECEMBER

REFLECT ON YOUR BEGINNER'S MIND

What do you see in the mirror? Instead of focusing on your perceived flaws, switch to a nonjudgmental "beginner's mind," where everything looks new and welcoming.

11

MANAGE YOUR STRESS

Stress management is an important element of self-esteem. To understand its importance, visualize a guitar. If you tighten the strings too much, they will snap, but if you don't tighten them enough, they won't sound right. Tightening the strings with just the right tension will allow you to play beautiful music. Treat the stress you can manage in your life as music to your ears, as long as it is in balance.

12

DECEMBER

MISTAKES DON'T DEFINE YOU

Remember that you are a good and beautiful person no matter how many times you fall short. Mistakes are inevitable; beating yourself up about them is optional.

13

TAKE A RELAXATION BREAK

Relaxation exercises help you become more mindful. Give yourself a relaxation break for a few minutes a couple times today. This is especially helpful during busy times of the year. Breathe in through your nose slowly, and then slowly let your breath out through your mouth. Allow a word like "peace," "love," or "calm" to come to mind, and repeat it throughout the break. When your mind begins to wander, just note it rather than react to it.

14

DECEMBER

AN AFFIRMATION FOR BEING YOUR BEST

I strive to be the best version of myself—it is so much better than trying to be any version of someone else.

15

SELF-CARE IS NOT SELFISH

Self-care is not selfish—it involves taking care of yourself enough so that you see you are as important as everyone else. When you take care of yourself, everyone benefits!

16

DECEMBER

DEVELOP STRONG CONNECTIONS

Think of how you can improve on the strength of your people connections. The quality of our support system often correlates with how we feel about ourselves. While no one can give us self-esteem, having strong, supportive familial and friendship bonds provides invaluable support to our mental health. When you feel stressed, don't isolate—connect!

17

DECEMBER

THANK YOURSELF

We often think nothing of thanking others. What if you took the time today to thank yourself? Are you thankful for your perseverance, your kindness to others, your courage to go on after adversity, or your ability to let go of someone close to you who was not healthy for you? Reflect on the many things to thank yourself for.

18

DECEMBER

REFLECT, RESET, REFRESH, AND REJUVENATE

Take time out to *reflect* on what you learned this year and what you would like to do differently next year. Consider how you can *reset* your priorities based on what you know now, and *refresh* your mind with thinking about possibilities and new perspectives. *Rejuvenate* yourself with a "beginner's mind," seeking to become more mindful with new ways of looking at things. Energize yourself to make this season and new year the best!

19

BE AT PEACE WITH YOURSELF

Choose to be at peace with yourself for who you are right at this moment. Release yourself from self-doubt, and trust the path you have taken in your life. Take comfort in the fact that you are doing your best, trying your best, and making the best out of what comes your way. Never doubt your greatness for one moment.

20
DECEMBER

AN AFFIRMATION FOR SELF-LOVE

Unconditional self-love doesn't just happen to me. It is something I choose to practice each day.

21

MAKE SURE YOUR AFFIRMATIONS ARE POSITIVE

If you started this book from the beginning, have you been following the suggestion on January 2 (page 2) about writing a daily positive affirmation? If not, there is no better time to start than now! Make sure they are indeed positive, though. For example, "I will do great at my presentation" is not really positive—it puts too much pressure on success. Rather, "I am proud of how I am preparing" is much more achievable and less judgmental.

SELF-COMPASSION LEADS TO HIGHER SELF-ESTEEM

The first thing to know is that self-compassion and self-esteem do tend to go together.

—KRISTIN NEFF

23

WRITE YOURSELF A LETTER

As you reflect on the past year, write yourself a letter about what you have learned, what you have accomplished, what you are proud of, what you would like to improve on, and define some goals for the upcoming year.

Seal the letter in an envelope and open it up in the new year to remind yourself of everything you've done. Consider actually mailing it yourself for even more of an impact!

24

DECEMBER

BE THANKFUL FOR YOUR LIFE

Today, be grateful for everything good that life has given you. Start the day off right with a big thank-you!

25

THE BEST GIFTS TO GIVE

Today, remember that the best gifts you can give to others are free. Make sure to give them to yourself, too!

Love

Empathy

Forgiveness

Respect

Acceptance

Support

26

MAKE YOUR GOALS BIG

Self-esteem is correlated with helping and contributing to others, causes you believe in, and in the world outside yourself. Whether it is through work, volunteerism, raising children, coaching a youth team, etc., the more you commit to achieving goals bigger than yourself, the more you will get in return. Think of some of the goals you presently pursue, and others that you would like to commit to in the future. How can you make them bigger than yourself? How can your goals help your community?

27

DECEMBER

FINANCIAL SELF-CARE

In this gift-giving season, when budgets are often stretched, take an inventory of your financial health. If you are spending over your means, your self-esteem will suffer. Are you living too much on credit? Do you have a savings plan and money for unexpected expenses? Take time today to figure out short-term and long-term goals for your financial self-care.

28

DECEMBER

YOU DID THE BEST YOU COULD

Instead of beating yourself up for actions you regret, focus on the hurt that led you to make missteps, and find soothing words for your younger self.

29

DECEMBER

FORGIVE THEM

In this gift-giving season, give someone the gift of forgiveness, especially when they can't forgive themselves.

30

SELF-ESTEEM "MUSTS"

As this year ends and the new year begins, reflect on the choices you have made and the choices you have in front of you. Commit to choosing the healthier alternatives. Consider writing in a journal or in a note on your smartphone the choices you want to make to start the new year off right. The following are some ideas of the choices you have. You can choose:

- Love over judgment
- Connection over isolation
- Acceptance over bitterness
- Forgiveness over grudges
- Healing over loss
- Learning over stagnation
- Optimism over pessimism

31

ARE YOUR GOALS SMART?

SMART goals offer an acronym to help us be more productive and effective in all areas of our lives. Use this acronym to start the year off right by making your goals SMART. An example of a SMART goal would be:

Specific: I will walk four times a week for at least 5,000 steps.

Measurable: I will use my fitness watch to measure the time and steps.

Action-oriented/achievable: I've committed time to the plan and got new sneakers.

Relevant: It will boost my health and self-esteem.

Time-bound: I will do this for one month and then reassess my goals.

Think of one SMART goal today with this acronym as your guide.

Resources

BOOKS

A Guide to Rational Living by Albert Ellis and Robert A. Harper
A landmark book that laid the groundwork for the foundation of cognitive behavioral therapy.

A Year of Positive Thinking: Daily Inspiration, Wisdom, and Courage
by Cyndie Spiegel
This delightful book offers 365 days of positive thinking and helps readers change their thoughts to change their lives.

A Year of Self-Care: Daily Practices and Inspiration for Caring for Yourself
by Dr. Zoe Shaw
This wonderful book offers 365 days of self-care tips, practices, and inspirational messages to help you take care of your mind, body, and spirit.

Embrace Your Greatness: 50 Ways to Build Unshakeable Self-Esteem
by Judith Belmont
In this book, you'll find powerful—yet incredibly simple—tools grounded in mindfulness, acceptance, self-compassion, and positive psychology to help you start feeling good about yourself.

Get Out of Your Mind and Into Your Life: The New Acceptance and Commitment Therapy by Steven C. Hayes and Spencer Smith
A valuable workbook offering explanations and practices for acceptance and commitment therapy.

Learned Optimism: How to Change Your Mind and Your Life by Martin Seligman
By the originator of positive psychology, this book helps readers use principles of positive psychology to improve their sense of well-being and happiness.

Mindfulness Skills for Kids: Card Deck and 3 Card Games by Debra Burdick
This colorful and fun therapeutic card deck offers parents, teachers, and clinicians a great tool to help children learn mindfulness techniques.

Self-Compassion: The Proven Power of Being Kind to Yourself by Kristin Neff
An important book about the significance of self-compassion in the development of true, long-lasting self-esteem.

Self-Esteem: A Proven Program of Cognitive Techniques for Assessing, Improving, and Maintaining Your Self-Esteem by Matthew McKay
A classic book about self-esteem, highlighting practical cognitive strategies to improve self-esteem.

Self-Love Workbook for Women: Release Self-Doubt, Build Self-Compassion, and Embrace Who You Are by Megan Logan
This colorful workbook helps women build self-compassion and self-love.

Ten Days to Self-Esteem by David Burns
A wonderful book by acclaimed psychologist David Burns teaching practical cognitive behavioral therapy techniques to improve self-esteem.

The Anxiety and Stress Solution Deck: 55 CBT and Mindfulness Tips and Tools
by Judith Belmont
These easy-to-use cards offer practical strategies to manage stress and anxiety. Each card offers a quick tip, followed by a tool, a short activity to put that tip into practice, and a takeaway.

Tips and Tools for the Therapeutic Toolbox series by Judith Belmont
This four-book series offers various tools such as reproducible handouts, worksheets, and activities for therapists to use with their clients on different mental health and wellness topics.

You Are a Badass: How to Stop Doubting Your Greatness and Start Living an Awesome Life by Jen Sincero
A fun and clever book on how to live your best life.

WEBSITES

Belmont Wellness: BelmontWellness.com
This is my website, offering free resources such as handouts and worksheets for various mental health and wellness topics.

Marc and Angel Hack Life: MarcAndAngel.com
This website has great blog posts about many areas of personal growth and emotional wellness, offering powerful insights and tools for growth.

Psych Central: PsychCentral.com
Psych Central offers a variety of mental health resources, including blog posts, self-tests and quizzes, and podcasts, as well as information on a variety of mental health disorders and wellness issues. The site is overseen by mental health professionals.

Self-Thrive: SelfThrive.com
This website offers a variety of blog posts on areas of wellness, positivity, productivity, relationships, and many other areas of personal development.

Steven Aitchison: StevenAitchison.co.uk
This inspirational website has a variety of upbeat blog posts about various personal development issues such as personal growth, health, relationships, business, and spirituality.

References

Angelo, Megan. "9 Things Lucille Ball Taught Us about Life." *Glamour*. August 6, 2013. www.glamour.com/story/lucille-ball.

Angelou, Maya. *Letter to My Daughter*. New York: Random House, 2008.

Carlson, Richard. *Don't Sweat the Small Stuff . . . and It's All Small Stuff: Simple Ways to Keep the Little Things from Taking Over Your Life*. New York: Hyperion, 1997.

Carnegie, Dale. *How to Stop Worrying and Start Living: Time-Tested Methods for Conquering Worry*. New York: Gallery Books, 2004.

Clemens, Samuel. *What Is Man? And Other Stories*. De Vinne Press, 1906. Urbana, IL: Project Gutenberg, May 11, 2009. Last updated February 24, 2018. e-book. www.gutenberg.org/files/70/70-h/70-h.htm.

Crane, Frank. *Adventures in Common Sense*. New York: John Lane Company, 1916.

Dyer, Wayne W. *Everyday Wisdom for Success*. Carlsbad, CA: Hay House, 2006.

Dyer, Wayne W. *Staying on the Path*. Carlsbad, CA: Hay House, 1995.

Elliot, Cabot James. *A Memoir of Ralph Waldo Emerson*. Vol. 2. Cambridge, MA: Riverside Press, 1887.

Epstein, Joseph. *The Yale Book of Quotations*. New Haven, CT: Yale University Press, 2006.

Germer, Christopher K. *The Mindful Path to Self-Compassion: Freeing Yourself from Destructive Thoughts and Emotions.* New York: Guilford Press, 2009.

Hanson, Rick. *Hardwiring Happiness: The New Brain Science of Contentment, Calm, and Confidence.* New York: Harmony Books, 2013.

Hay, Louise L. *You Can Heal Your Life.* Carlsbad, CA: Hay House, 2016.

Hyams, Joe. *Zen in the Martial Arts.* New York: Bantam, 1982.

Kushner, Harold S. *Overcoming Life's Disappointments: Learning from Moses How to Cope with Frustration.* New York: Anchor Books, 2007.

Neff, Kristin. *Self-Compassion: The Proven Power of Being Kind to Yourself.* New York: William Morrow, 2015.

Neff, Kristin. "Why Self-Compassion Trumps Self-Esteem." Greater Good. Accessed April 16, 2021. greatergood.berkeley.edu/article/item/try _selfcompassion.

"Perspectives on Pearl Harbor: Apologies Across the Pacific?: America and Japan Each Had a Day of Infamy, and Should Take This Occasion as an Opportunity to Admit the Wrong." *Los Angeles Times.* December 2, 1991. www.latimes.com /archives/la-xpm-1991-12-02-me-530-story.html.

Rogers, Fred. *You Are Special: Neighborly Words of Wisdom from Mister Rogers.* New York: Penguin Books, 1995.

Schulz, Kathryn. "Don't Regret Regret." TED Talk, 16:10. November 2011. www.ted.com/talks/kathryn_schulz_don_t_regret_regret?language=en.

Seligman, Martin E. P. *What You Can Change and What You Can't: The Complete Guide to Successful Self-Improvement*. New York: Vintage Books, 2007.

Smithsonian Institution. "Patsy Sherman: Scotchguard™ Inventor." Lemelson Center for the Study of Invention and Innovation, May 12, 2014. invention.si.edu/node/1145/p/430-patsy-sherman-scotchgard-inventor#:~:text=In%201952%20an%20assistant%20in,use%20in%20aircraft%20fuel%20lines.

Steinem, Gloria. *Revolution from Within: A Book of Self-Esteem*. New York: Little, Brown and Company, 1994.

Winfrey, Oprah. *What I Know for Sure*. New York: Flatiron Books, 2014.

Winfrey, Oprah. "What I Know for Sure." Oprah.com. Accessed April 22, 2021. www.oprah.com/omagazine/what-i-know-for-sure-oprah-winfrey/all#:~:text=%22Self%2Desteem%20comes%20from%20being,worthwhile%20if%20you%20inhibit%20yourself.%22&text=%22Use%20what%20you%20have%20to,I%20now%20live%20my%20life.%22.

Acknowledgments

I have gained so much from the experts in the psychology field who have provided a wealth of information on self-help strategies and information. The work of CBT pioneers Aaron Beck, Albert Ellis, and David Burns; Kristin Neff's work on self-compassion; Steven Hayes's acceptance and commitment therapy strategies; and Martin Seligman's work in the field of positive psychology with its focus on wellness strategies, have all been very influential. I am truly indebted to them.

Most of all, I am grateful for my husband, Don, who has supported me on every step of my life journey. I am truly grateful for the wonderful husband, father, and grandfather you are. My love for you just keeps on growing.

About the Author

Judith Belmont, MS, graduated from the University of Pennsylvania with a BS in psychology, and Hahnemann Medical College with an MS in clinical psychology. She is the author of eight mental health and wellness books and two therapeutic card decks. She is a retired licensed psychotherapist, and presently offers online mental health coaching, as well as online webinars and workplace wellness presentations.

Judith lives in southwest Florida and in southern New Jersey in the summer. Find out more at belmontwellness.com.

CPSIA information can be obtained
at www.ICGtesting.com
Printed in the USA
JSHW011907280122
22324JS00001B/1

9 781638 073406